SpringerBriefs in Education

We are delighted to announce SpringerBriefs in Education, an innovative product type that combines elements of both journals and books. Briefs present concise summaries of cutting-edge research and practical applications in education. Featuring compact volumes of 50 to 125 pages, the SpringerBriefs in Education allow authors to present their ideas and readers to absorb them with a minimal time investment. Briefs are published as part of Springer's eBook Collection. In addition, Briefs are available for individual print and electronic purchase.

SpringerBriefs in Education cover a broad range of educational fields such as: Science Education, Higher Education, Educational Psychology, Assessment & Evaluation, Language Education, Mathematics Education, Educational Technology, Medical Education and Educational Policy.

SpringerBriefs typically offer an outlet for:

- An introduction to a (sub)field in education summarizing and giving an overview of theories, issues, core concepts and/or key literature in a particular field
- A timely report of state-of-the art analytical techniques and instruments in the field of educational research
- A presentation of core educational concepts
- An overview of a testing and evaluation method
- A snapshot of a hot or emerging topic or policy change
- An in-depth case study
- A literature review
- A report/review study of a survey
- An elaborated thesis

Both solicited and unsolicited manuscripts are considered for publication in the SpringerBriefs in Education series. Potential authors are warmly invited to complete and submit the Briefs Author Proposal form. All projects will be submitted to editorial review by editorial advisors.

SpringerBriefs are characterized by expedited production schedules with the aim for publication 8 to 12 weeks after acceptance and fast, global electronic dissemination through our online platform SpringerLink. The standard concise author contracts guarantee that:

- an individual ISBN is assigned to each manuscript
- each manuscript is copyrighted in the name of the author
- the author retains the right to post the pre-publication version on his/her website or that of his/her institution

Xibin Han · Qian Zhou · Ming Li · Yuping Wang
Editors

Handbook of Technical and Vocational Teacher Professional Development in the Digital Age

Springer

Editors
Xibin Han
Institute of Education
Tsinghua University
Beijing, China

Qian Zhou
Institute of Education
Tsinghua University
Beijing, China

Ming Li
The International Centre for Higher
Education Innovation under the auspices
of UNESCO
Southern University of Science
and Technology
Shenzhen, Guangdong, China

Yuping Wang
School of Humanities, Languages
and Social Science
Griffith University
Brisbane, QLD, Australia

ISSN 2211-1921　　　　　　　　ISSN 2211-193X　(electronic)
SpringerBriefs in Education
ISBN 978-981-99-5936-5　　　　ISBN 978-981-99-5937-2　(eBook)
https://doi.org/10.1007/978-981-99-5937-2

© The Rightsholder (if applicable) and The Author(s) 2024. This book is an open access publication.

Open Access This book is licensed under the terms of the Creative Commons Attribution-NonCommercial-NoDerivatives 4.0 International License (http://creativecommons.org/licenses/by-nc-nd/4.0/), which permits any noncommercial use, sharing, distribution and reproduction in any medium or format, as long as you give appropriate credit to the original author(s) and the source, provide a link to the Creative Commons license and indicate if you modified the licensed material. You do not have permission under this license to share adapted material derived from this book or parts of it.

The images or other third party material in this book are included in the book's Creative Commons license, unless indicated otherwise in a credit line to the material. If material is not included in the book's Creative Commons license and your intended use is not permitted by statutory regulation or exceeds the permitted use, you will need to obtain permission directly from the copyright holder.

This work is subject to copyright. All commercial rights are reserved by the author(s), whether the whole or part of the material is concerned, specifically the rights of translation, reprinting, reuse of illustrations, recitation, broadcasting, reproduction on microfilms or in any other physical way, and transmission or information storage and retrieval, electronic adaptation, computer software, or by similar or dissimilar methodology now known or hereafter developed. Regarding these commercial rights a non-exclusive license has been granted to the publisher.

The use of general descriptive names, registered names, trademarks, service marks, etc. in this publication does not imply, even in the absence of a specific statement, that such names are exempt from the relevant protective laws and regulations and therefore free for general use.

The publisher, the authors, and the editors are safe to assume that the advice and information in this book are believed to be true and accurate at the date of publication. Neither the publisher nor the authors or the editors give a warranty, expressed or implied, with respect to the material contained herein or for any errors or omissions that may have been made. The publisher remains neutral with regard to jurisdictional claims in published maps and institutional affiliations.

This Springer imprint is published by the registered company Springer Nature Singapore Pte Ltd.
The registered company address is: 152 Beach Road, #21-01/04 Gateway East, Singapore 189721, Singapore

Paper in this product is recyclable.

Foreword

The advancements of digital technologies such as artificial intelligence, blockchains, quantum computing and the fifth generation of mobile communication technology (5G) have dramatically transformed our lives and the world of work today. Such a transformation is not only changing the way we live, but also the way we think and communicate. Digital thinking, distributed cognition, knowledge dissemination and interpersonal communication in virtual spaces are just some of the examples. As far as the future world of work is concerned, the digitalization of industry and industrialization of digital technologies have gone hand in hand to accelerate the transformative process of reskilling and upskilling of the workforce today. In return, the transformation occurring industry has motivated a comprehensive and systematic evolution of the ways we foster and nurture the capacity of future workforce. Digital transformation of technical and vocational education and training (TVET) is inevitable, and TVET teachers need to respond to it urgently.

This is the large context in which this handbook was proposed and written. It constitutes part of a large-scaled international research project on the digital transformation happening in education. This project publishes one report and three handbooks, namely the *Research Report on Digital Transformation of Higher Education Teaching and Learning*, the *Handbook of Technical and Vocational Teacher Professional Development in the Digital Age*, the *Handbook of Teaching Competencies Development in Higher Education* and the *Handbook of Educational Reform through Blended Learning*.

These publications are a culmination of the expertise of more than 50 educational technology and TVET professionals from across the world, under the guidance and supervision of the International Centre for Higher Education Innovation under the auspices of UNSCO (Shenzhen, China) and Institute of Education, Tsinghua University, China.

We hope, this handbook, the *Handbook of Technical and Vocational Teacher Professional Development in the Digital Age*, will serve as a useful reference for the government departments and TVET institutions to inform policymaking and strategic decisions in regard to teacher professional development. It will also provide a practice toolkit for TVET teachers when developing and assessing their professional competencies. The insights and practical recommendations contained in this book will contribute to the development of highly competent TVET teachers who are equipped with the vision, values, knowledge and skills needed for the digital age. They, in turn, will speed up the digital transformation of TVET and ensure the quality and relevance of TVET.

There are five chapters to this handbook. It starts with an introduction of the context in which this research was conducted, highlighting the need for further research into TVET teachers' professional development in the digital age. To this end, the introduction situates TVET teachers' professional development in the context of digital transformation in Industry 4.0 era. It further exposits how TVET teachers' professional development relates and interrelates with the digital transformation of TVET, and how and why it should be supported by the integration of technology such as AI and theories such as lifelong learning. Chapter 1 is followed by a review of key theories and approaches to teacher professional growth in Chap. 2. These theories provide a theoretical underpinning for the proposal of TVET teachers' digital competency framework in Chap. 3. This framework is particularly built on a discussion of the roles that TVET teachers are expected to play in the time of TVET digital transformation and reform. It highlights the competencies needed for developing the dual quality of TVET professionals, that is, being both a knowledge provider and a vocational skill trainer. The second part of Chap. 3 develops a set of comprehensive indicators for each of the competencies proposed in the framework. These indicators are further developed to become an assessment tool for evaluating TVET teachers' competencies in the digital age. Chapter 4 adopts an ecological approach to view teacher professional growth as an ecological system with different components feeding into one another. These components can include national/international, institutional and individual efforts and strategies, resources, technologies and modes of learning. Guided by this approach, this chapter reviews the policies, strategies and achievements made by international and national organizations, institutions and individual teachers throughout the world. The book concludes with the presentation of exemplary cases of teacher professional development practice in Chap. 5, which could be an inspiring resource for policymakers and TVET professionals.

This handbook was edited by Xibin Han, Qian Zhou, Ming Li and Yuping Wang. We would like to recognize the contributions of the following team of scholars who generously provided insightful input to the compilation of this handbook. Jiangang Cheng, Jihua Song, Xiaojing Bai, Yangyang Luo, Meng Li and Xiangyu Chen wrote different parts in the Chinese version of Chap. 1. The information contained in this chapter informed the English writing of the current Chap. 1 in this book by Yuping Wang. The Chinese version of Chap. 2 was drafted by Jihua Song, Zhixian Zhong, Chun He, and Hongyan Lu and Xibin Han. Based on the English translation of this chapter by Xibei Xiong, Yuping Wang edited and rewrote parts of this chapter in English. Chapter 3 was written in Chinese and translated into English by Junfeng Diao, Xibin Han and Qian Zhou. It was edited and rewritten by Yuping Wang. Qian Zhou, Junfeng Diao, Mingxuan Chen, Chengming Yang, Mei Li, Jing Wang, Kaiyu Yi and Xibin Han drafted Chap. 4 in Chinese, which was translated into English by Guanqiang Cui and edited by Tiedao Zhang and Yuping Wang. The Chinese version of Chap. 5 was compiled by Tiedao Zhang, Qian Zhou, Chengming Yang, Xiaojing Bai and Xibin Han and was translated into English by Guoqiang Cui, Tiedao Zhang and Yuping Wang. The English version was edited by Tiedao Zhang and Yuping Wang. The final draft of the book was edited and reviewed by Yuping Wang and proofread by Taralynn Hartsell.

Special thanks also go to Qingyu Jiang, etc. of the International Centre for Higher Education Innovation under the auspices of UNSCO (Shenzhen, China); Yingqun Liu, Rifa Guo, Wanruo Shi and Jingjng Liu of Institute of Education, Tsinghua University; and Zhenyu Deng, Xiaofen Shi, Huanle Zhu, Yi Zhang, Yuhong Zhao, Yiling Liang and Niu He of Jinagxi Normal University for their continuous support. Last but most importantly, we would like to express our sincere appreciation of the support and contributions from all of the TVET institutions and teachers involved in this project. Without their years of tremendous achievements in TVET research and practice, this book would not exist.

Jiangang Cheng
Director of Institute of Higher Education Digital
Transformation of UNESCO-ICHEI
Professor of Institute of Education
Tsinghua University
Beijing, China

Contents

1 **Introduction** 1
   Yuping Wang, Jiangang Cheng, Jihua Song, Xiaojing Bai,
   Yangyang Luo, Meng Li, and Xiangyu Chen

2 **Definitions and a Review of Relevant Theories, Frameworks,
   and Approaches** 17
   Jihua Song, Zhixian Zhong, Chun He, Hongyan Lu, Xibin Han,
   Xibei Xiong, and Yuping Wang

3 **Professional Competencies in TVET: Framework, Indicators
   and Assessment Instrument** 41
   Junfeng Diao, Xibin Han, Qian Zhou, and Yuping Wang

4 **Strategies for Developing TVET Teachers' Professional
   Competencies** 75
   Qian Zhou, Junfeng Diao, Yuping Wang, Mingxuan Chen,
   Chengming Yang, Mei Li, Jing Wang, Kaiyu Yi, Xibin Han,
   Guoqiang Cui, and Tiedao Zhang

5 **Exemplars of Good Practice** 91
   Tiedao Zhang, Qian Zhou, Chengming Yang, Xiaojing Bai,
   Xibin Han, Guoqiang Cui, and Yuping Wang

Glossary of Terms 121

Contributors

Xiaojing Bai Beijing Open University, Beijing, China

Mingxuan Chen School of Humanities, Jiangnan University, Wuxi, China

Xiangyu Chen Institute of Education, Tsinghua University, Beijing, China

Jiangang Cheng Institute of Education, Tsinghua University, Beijing, China

Guoqiang Cui Villanova Institute for Teaching and Learning, Villanova University, Villanova, PA, USA

Junfeng Diao School of Education, Hainan Normal University, Haikou, China

Xibin Han Institute of Education, Tsinghua University, Beijing, China

Chun He School of Artificial Intelligence, Beijing Normal University, Beijing, China

Mei Li Beijing Open University, Beijing, China

Meng Li Institute of Education, Tsinghua University, Beijing, China

Hongyan Lu Institute of Teacher Education for Advanced Study, Jiangxi Normal University, Nanchang, China

Yangyang Luo Institute of Higher Education, Lanzhou University, Lanzhou, China

Jihua Song School of Artificial Intelligence, Beijing Normal University, Beijing, China

Jing Wang School of Humanities, Jiangnan University, Wuxi, China

Yuping Wang School of Humanities, Languages and Social Science, Griffith University, Brisbane, Australia

Xibei Xiong School of Education, Guangxi Normal University, Guilin, China

Chengming Yang Graduate School of Education, Beijing Foreign Studies University, Beijing, China

Kaiyu Yi Institute of Education, Tsinghua University, Beijing, China

Tiedao Zhang Beijing Open University, Beijing, China

Zhixian Zhong Institute of Teacher Education for Advanced Study, Jiangxi Normal University, Nanchang, China

Qian Zhou Institute of Education, Tsinghua University, Beijing, China

Chapter 1
Introduction

Yuping Wang, Jiangang Cheng, Jihua Song, Xiaojing Bai, Yangyang Luo, Meng Li, and Xiangyu Chen

> You give a man a fish and you feed him for a day. You teach him to fish and you give him an occupation that will feed him for a lifetime.
> —A Chinese Proverb

1.1 Background

It is not an exaggeration to say that technology has transformed all fronts of our society. Technologies such as Artificial Intelligent (AI), virtual reality, cloud computing, blockchain, and quantum computing have changed how we live, how we communicate, how we learn, how we work and even how we think. The boundary between the physical and virtual worlds is becoming increasingly blurred, so much so that the arrival of Industry 4.0 has been announced (Schwab, 2016) and embraced by industry. The term 'metaverse' has emerged as a catchword of 2022. At the same time, the Covid-19 pandemic has delivered us another global disruption that has no historical precedent. The whole world seemed to be in a disruptive state. No one can

---

Y. Wang (✉)
School of Humanities, Languages and Social Science, Griffith University, Brisbane, Australia
e-mail: y.wang@griffith.edu.au

J. Cheng · M. Li · X. Chen
Institute of Education, Tsinghua University, Beijing, China

J. Song
School of Artificial Intelligence, Beijing Normal University, Beijing, China

X. Bai
Beijing Open University, Beijing, China

Y. Luo
Institute of Higher Education, Lanzhou University, Lanzhou, China

© The Author(s) 2024
X. Han et al. (eds.), *Handbook of Technical and Vocational Teacher Professional Development in the Digital Age*, SpringerBriefs in Education,
https://doi.org/10.1007/978-981-99-5937-2_1

precisely predict what the post-pandemic era holds for us but one thing is certain: the world has changed and is fast changing.

Technical and Vocational Education and Training (TVET), with its aim to help youth and adults develop values, attitude, knowledge and skills needed for the world of work, directly addresses the nexus between education and the world of work. Thus it is inevitably and strategically positioned at the forefront of post-pandemic recovery, transition and digital transformation. Put simply, in comparison to higher education, there is an urgency and immediacy in the challenges facing TVET in the post-pandemic era thanks to TVET's closer ties with workplace. These challenges can mean how to restructure the TVET system globally to ensure its relevancy. These challenges can also mean finding effective and efficient ways to help current and future workforce to identify skills and knowledge needed for transitioning to digital and green economies that is already happening. Similarly, providing urgently needed flexible pathways for developing these skills and knowledge can also be extremely challenging and pressing. More importantly, these challenges give rise to the exigency to cultivate the kind of mindset required for digital transformation, sustainable economies, social cohesion and justice. However, is TVET ready to rise to these challenges? How should TVET respond to digital transformation to stay relevant in the era recovery, transition and transformation? What competencies do TVET teachers need to contribute to the development of a new generation of workforce ready for economic recovery, digital transformation and Industry 4.0? In what ways can these competencies be developed and evaluated? These are the focal issues that this handbook explores with the aim to assist TVET teachers in their professional development as a lifelong learner.

1.2 Digital Transformation and Industry 4.0

The concept of Industry 4.0, also known as the Fourth Industrial Revolution, was first popularized by Professor Klaus Schwab, founder and executive Chairman of the World Economic Forum in 2015 (Philbeck & Davis, 2018; Schwab, 2016). This concept refers to the era starting at the turn of this century and was placed into a historical context of the first, second and third industrial revolutions. From a technological point view, all the four industrial revolutions have been driven by technological advancements. The First Industrial Revolution is commonly referred to as the period between 1760 and 1840 when water and steam power fundamentally changed production from being manual to mechanical. The Second Industrial Revolution occurring between 1871 and 1914 is also known as the technological revolution. It was marked by the use of electricity resulting in mass production and assembly lines. The invention of mainframe computers and semiconductors in the latter part of the Twentieth Century gave birth to the Third Industrial Revolution, which is also described as the digital revolution (Schwab, 2016). The development of personal computers in the 1970s and the Internet in the 1990s further advances this period into an age of automation of production. Although the Fourth Industrial

Revolution is regarded as being built on the Third, it is not commonly considered as an incremental advancement from the previous revolutions. When justifying the arrival of Industry 4.0, Schwab (2016) argued that the interruption brought about by digital technology is incomparable to the previous industrial revolutions in terms of its velocity, scope and systems impact. This is because a fusion of technologies such as AI, advanced robotics, 3D printing, quantum computing, internet of things and biotechnology have brought with them both innovations and disruptions to our lives in a unprecedented fashion. Emergent and emerging digital technologies are fundamentally changing our society, transforming productivity, communication and connectivity, and even blurring the boundaries between the physical, virtual, and biological worlds (Schwab, 2016). As far as industry is concerned, much more flexible and adaptive AI and computer-integrated production systems and the use of cyber-physical systems and cloud manufacturing might mean the replacement of human workers (for a detailed review and discussion on the impact of AI on skill development in the digital age, see Shiohira, 2021). This trend calls for a new workforce with multiple competencies and transversal skills, who can collaborate with both humans and technologies to solve complex technical problems in the production process (MacDougall, 2014; Madsen et al., 2016; Yu et al., 2015). More complex vocational skills and collaboration skills are needed in Industry 4.0 (MacDougall, 2014; Madsen et al., 2016). In turn, these changes can also dramatically influence social and environmental sustainable development (Bai et al., 2020).

1.3 Digital Transformation of TVET

As far as education is concerned, it is an established reality that today's learning, teaching and training have been transformed dramatically by technological advancements. How should TVET, as "a pathway for individuals to thrive, a catalyst towards sustainable economies, and a vector of social justice" (UNESCO TVET Strategy for 2022–2029), respond to the challenges and opportunities brought about by the digital transformation occurring in Industry 4.0?

As suggested by the term of TVET, vocational education consists of both domain knowledge learning and vocational skills learning and training. The arrival of the Industry 4.0 era is not only outdating some of the domain knowledge, occupations and skills, but also creating new values, knowledge and disciplinary areas that compel TVET to prepare the future workforce for. Therefore, such a transformation calls for a more urgent response from TVET to keep up with the rapidly changing industry needs. TVET must be reformed in many significant ways to stay relevant. Digitizing is one thing and transformation is another. To be more specific, digital transformation of TVET does not just mean the digitization of learning contents, nor does it merely mean the adoption of digital technologies to support learning, assessment and skill training. More importantly, it means the transformation of what and how students learn, what and how teachers teach and what and how trainers train. This is a process in which technology should be seamlessly integrated with pedagogy to innovate teaching and training, and in some cases, this can mean an overhaul of an entire curriculum in order to equip future workforce with the values, knowledge and skills needed to survive in the digital age. In this transformative process, learning becomes deeper, broader, more transversal and richer in content and more effective, diverse and flexible in mode. As ILO Centenary Declaration for the Future of Work (ILO, 2019) put it, a 'human-centred approach to the future of work' and 'effective lifelong learning and quality education for all' are needed to ensure the success of such a transformation. So much so repeated calls for re-examine and reinvigorate education has been heard from both academics and policy makers. For example, Zaharah et al. (2018) reviewed research published between 2015 and 2018 on the topic of TVET in the era of Industrial 4.0 and their findings are still relevant today. Confirming the persistent challenges specific to TVET, such as quality, relevance, financing and attractiveness, their review specified the need for TVET to re-audit and re-examine curricula and program outputs in order to stay relevant to industrial needs in Industry 4.0 (Ali & Abdulkadir, 2017; Sommer & Kreibich, 2017; World Economic Forum, 2017). The *Beijing Consensus on Artificial Intelligence and Education* (UNESCO, 2019) also calls for the use of AI to empower teaching and learning so as to develop students' interdisciplinary skills and competencies and make the learning process more adaptive.

In view of these transformative needs and changes, UNESCO, in most of its strategic initiatives and policy statements regarding TVET, highlights the importance of equipping all youth and adults with relevant knowledge, skills and competencies for work, life, and entrepreneurships. Lifelong learning has been emphasized as an important pathway to stay relevant to sustainable industrial and societal developments (UNESCO, 2016; UNESCO Strategy for TVET (2016–2021)). The recently published UNESCO TVET Strategy for 2022–2029 continues to prioritise the development of skills for individuals to learn, work and live, for economies to transition towards sustainable development and for societies to become more inclusive and resilient (UNESCO TVET Strategy for 2022–2029).

In the last 20 years, different levels of efforts have been made throughout the world to ready TVET for the digital transformation happening in the workplace. UNESCO has set us a great example in this regard by accelerating its efforts in promoting the quality of TVET globally since the turn of the century. These efforts can be exemplified in its International Congresses on TVET held every four years and the development of a five-year strategy for TVET since 2010 (e.g., UNESCO Strategy for TVET (2010–2015) and UNSCO Strategy for TVET (2016–2021)). The new Strategy for TVET (2022–2029) was just released at a hybrid international conference in October, 2022 at the UNESCO-UNEVOC International Centre for TVET in Bonn, Germany. These strategic documents aim to contribute to the adoption and implementation of Sustainable Development Goal 4 and the Education 2030 Framework for Action. Another exemplary effort by UNESCO is the establishment of more than 250 UNESCO UNEVOC Centres in 166 UNESCO Member States since 1993. Its purpose is stated in the mission statement, "As UNESCO's designated centre for technical and vocational education and training (TVET), UNESCO-UNEVOC supports Member States in their efforts to strengthen and upgrade their

TVET systems" (UNESCO-UNEVOC, 2022a). Since 2016, the centre's leadership program has trained 654 TVET leaders, managers and staff from 112 countries. In addressing TVET's recovery from the impact of the Covid-19 pandemic, the leadership program in 2021 featured the theme of "Skills for the digital transformation: How TVET institutions can respond to future demands" (UNESCO-UNEVOC, 2022b).

In Europe, CEDEFOP, the European Centre for the Development of Vocational Education and Training, has made consistent efforts in assisting the European Union and its member nations to promote creativity, innovation and entrepreneurship in vocational education and training, and create professional development opportunities for TVET teachers and trainers (CEDEFOP, 2015). Since its inception in 1975, the centre has provided policy consultation to the EU and enhanced the dissemination and sharing of knowledge and good practices in vocational education and training among EU member states (https://www.cedefop.europa.eu/en/about-cedefop/what-we-do). One recent example is the establishment of the CEDEFOP Community of Learning Providers. This is a platform for EU TVET community and CEDEFOP to share and promote good practices, provide strategic consultation and guidance, and feed into general EU Commission policy (CEDEFOP, 2019).

In China, TVET is the main source of skilled workforce. China's TVET institutions are largely state-run. There are three types of provision: junior secondary, senior secondary and tertiary, with senior secondary institutions being the backbone of vocational education and training. There are 13,093 vocational institutions at this level, providing half of TVET graduates for China each year (Wang & Han, 2017). A top-down approach has been taken to promote vocational education throughout the country as evidenced in the issuing of series of state policies regarding TVET in the last 10 years. For example, in 2014, the State Council in China issued the 'z' (China G20, 2014), and the State Council of China (2019) published 'the National Implementation Plan for the Reform of Vocational Education'. The top-down approach was also taken at an institutional level in implementing institution-wide reforms such as blended learning adoption and digital campuses building. Strong institutional involvement was manifested in systematic policy, structure and strategy support (Han & Wang, 2021; Wang & Han, 2017). As a result, TVET in China has grown exponentially in the past decade to become one of the largest TVET providers in the world. In 2021, the enrolment for Senior high vocational schools reached 5.57million, 1.8 times higher than that in 2011. Secondary vocation schools also attracted 4.89 million enrolment in 2021. The combined graduates from senior high and secondary vocational schools reached 10 million every year (Ministry of Education of China, 2022b). In 2021, China had 1.29 million TVET teachers, an increase of 17% compared to the number of TVET teachers in 2012 (Ministry of Education of China, 2022b).

1.4 TVET Teachers' Professional Development in Industry 4.0

It has been widely acknowledged that teachers and trainers are the key change agents in fostering the capabilities of future workforce who can take on the challenges and make the best of the opportunities created by digital transformation (Jafar et al., 2020; Johnson et al., 2016; Latchem, 2017). In other words, how and how successfully TVET responds to the above-mentioned challenges and harnesses the potential of what digital transformation can offer largely depends on the competencies of TVET teachers and trainers. Are TVET teachers ready to help TVET to stay relevant to Industry 4.0? What competencies do they need to develop and how should they develop them effectively and in a sustainable manner?

1.4.1 What Competencies Are Required of TVET Teachers and Trainers in the Digital Age?

Our review of the research into TVET teachers' professional development indicates that a number of competency standards and frameworks for TVET teachers have been proposed to guide the professional development of pre-service and in-service teachers (see Diao & Yang, 2021; Diep & Hartmann, 2016; Jafar et al., 2020; Latchem, 2017; Wagiran et al., 2019). Despite all these efforts, in-service TVET teachers are still facing tremendous challenges in their professional development today as shown in the recent UNESCO trends mapping study (UNESCO-UNEVOC, 2022b). These challenges range from inadequate support in terms of infrastructure and resources, to the lack of adequate and effective professional development programs to help teachers develop digital competence. In fact, the shortage of teachers trained for quality vocational teaching and training and the lack of TVET facilities and infrastructure have been recognized as ongoing issues (Milio et al., 2014; World Economic Forum, 2017).

In the trends mapping study conducted by UNESCO-UNEVOC (2020), ten trends were mapped out in regard to teaching in TVET for the next ten years. They include the need for TVET graduates with transversal skills such as critical thinking and collaboration skills, and applied vocational skills, and the need for ongoing updating and upgrading of skills needed from industry. When exploring the key issues relating to the professional development of TVET teachers and trainers, this study highlights the importance of ongoing professional development and industry exposure for both in-service and pre-service TVET teachers and trainers. It also clearly specifies the need for developing teachers' and trainers' digital competencies focusing on building their digital skills, knowledge of new digital technologies, equipment and/or practices in the workplace. Most importantly, this study underscores the urgent need for TVET teachers to develop competencies in applying innovative pedagogical and technological approaches to the delivery of pedagogically sound teaching and training practices such as learner-centered teaching and training. These critical competencies are also aligned with the core competencies we propose in the competency framework for TVET teachers in the digital age, in Chap. 3 (see Sect. 3.2). In the proposed framework, we also attach great importance to the development of the dual role of TVET teachers being a knowledge provider and practical skill trainer. The need for developing TVET teachers' digital competencies is also underlined in this year's trends mapping study, which continues to call for further research into the "pedagogical skills and competencies needed to deliver high-quality, learner-centred, technology enhanced distance training in TVET" (UNESCO-UNEVOC, 2022b, p. 48). In China, policy support is strong and ongoing in the formulation of standards and frameworks for guiding teaching and learning reform in TVET and professional competency development. For example, in 2019, the Ministry of Education published the *Implementation Plan for Further Developing TVET Teachers' Dual Roles in the New Age* (Ministry of Education of China, 2019b), calling for a deeper reform of TVET, particularly in terms of the development of comprehensive professional standards and frameworks covering areas such as recruitment, promotion and performance evaluation. These areas were reiterated in the most recent policy statement, Notice Regarding the Promotion of TVET Teachers' Professional Competence (Ministry of Education of China, 2022a), issued by the Ministry of Education in May 2022. This Notice calls for further improving and normalizing professional standards for both TVET teachers and principals.

1.4.2 In What Ways Can TVET Teachers' Professional Competencies Be Fostered?

In this handbook, we advocate an ecological approach to TVET teachers' professional development as far as strategies are concerned. This approach sees teacher professional growth as the outcome of the concerted effort made at the national/international, institutional/industry and individual levels. These efforts complement one another. Only when they work together, can TVET teachers' lifelong agency growth be effective and sustained. In terms of mode of TVET teachers' professional development, we promote a diverse approach providing different and flexible pathways to support teacher professional growth, such as recognizing their personal efforts through a variety of certification systems (e.g., micro-credentials) and adopting a variety of technologies as support and enabling mechanisms.

Policy, Strategy and Structure Support

Policy support, national/global initiatives and guidance characterize the efforts of the national/international level strategies. Research has identified key areas to be targeted, such as improving the social status of TVET as a viable education pathway among learners, families, employers, policymakers and other stakeholders (Milio et al., 2014). Funding support should be provided to develop the most effective models of teacher training and professional development that meet the needs of Industrial 4.0 (World Economic Forum, 2017).

In the past 20 years, UNESCO has made consistent contributions in this regard, guiding TVET teaching globally through policies, initiatives and research findings such as trends mapping studies (UNESCO-UNEVOC, 2020, 2022b). For example, the four-stage model of technology integration in teaching proposed in *Improving the Quality of TVET Using Technology: A Practical Guide* (UNESCO-UNEVOC, 2020) has been widely used, presented a four-stage model of technology adoption, UNEVOC has also developed training initiatives and resources (e.g., training videos). According to the Discussion Document for UNESCO (2022) TVET Strategy for 2022–2029, between 2015 and 2021, UNESCO has trained more than 2700 TVET teachers around the world.

Countries around the world have also developed their own policies and frameworks regarding TVET teachers' professional competency development. For example, the COMET (Competence Development and Assessment in TVET) project originated in Germany has now become an international endeavour to develop and refine a competency and assessment model for both TVET students and teachers (see Sect. 2.2.2 for a more detailed discussion). In China, TVET teacher development features a top-down approach with government bodies at different levels playing key roles in policy making and funding support. For example, *The National Implementation Plan for the Reform of Vocational Education* published by the State Council of China (2019) proposes the establishment of 100 TVET teacher training bases throughout China to develop in-service teachers' dual competence as a class teacher and a vocational skill trainer. This plan also stipulates that in-service teachers need to be trained for at least one month every year either at the bases or in enterprises. Following this, the Ministry of Education has also issued various policy statements and strategic plans to provide systematic policy support for vocational teacher development. The Ministry's publication of A Strategy for TVET Teachers' Competency Development (2021–2025) is a case in point. Another effort unique to China's national efforts to promote TVET teacher development is the annual competition for Best ICT-Supported Teaching Practices. This competition is held at institutional, regional and national levels. (see Sect. 5.1).

At the institutional level, apart from policy and infrastructure support, ongoing and regular professional development programs and opportunities as well as incentives mechanisms dominate the efforts by TVET institutions and relevant departments within an institution throughout the world. In the Chinese TVET context, the cases discussed in Chaps. 4 and 5 and the TVET institutions investigated in Wang and Han (2017) and Han and Wang (2021) indicate that the institution is the key driver behind teacher professional development. All of these institutions adopted an institution-wide system-driven approach with clearly defined goals (e.g., promoting TVET teachers' dual role of being a knowledge provider and vocational skills trainer), coordinated programs and opportunities and concerted support at different levels within each institution. One unique feature to the Chinese TVET is that the institutions solicit external expertise (such as blended learning experts from higher education institutions) when developing and conducting their teacher professional development, especially at the beginning of their blended learning reforms (see Han & Wang, 2021; Wang & Han, 2017). Their experiences and achievements reveal a strong institutional role in TVET teachers' professional development.

Individual Efforts

As far as individual efforts are concerned, our ecological approach to teacher professional development places teachers in the centre of their professional development and sees teachers as the prime initiator of their own professional growth. Only when they are internally motivated and self-driven, can professional development be sustained and become a lifelong career growth path. Life-long learning and self-directed learning are particularly important to TVET teachers who are facing the double challenge of reiterative knowledge and skill updating and acceleration of new knowledge and skill acquisition, as necessitated by the fast changing industry needs. This challenge suggests that TVET teachers increasingly need to manage their own career trajectories through self-directed learning and evidencing their performance against the required professional standards. Fortunately, in the digital age, resources and technologies are at our fingertips (at least in developed and most developing countries) engendering flexible pathways for TVET teachers to become autonomous and life-long learners to stay relevant.

The digital age offers us abundant resources for teacher professional growth. Our research points to one of the most impactful resources for lifelong professional capacity building in the last decade, Open Educational Resources, commonly known as OERs. OERs refer to openly licensed materials that can be retained, reused, remixed, revised and redistributed (Open Educational Resources, n.d.; Wiley et al., 2018). OERs, contributing to equity, equality, quality, and inclusiveness, have proven to be an important alternative venue for teacher agency development and are regarded as the "catalysts of lifelong learning" and "continuous professional development" (Ossiannilsson, 2019, p. 131). However, as it was rightfully pointed out by Bossu and Willems (2017, p. 26), developing OER courses and resources alone was not enough for academic capacity building. Teachers' digital capacity to access OERs is a key to increase the use of OERs (for a detailed discussion of OERs, please see Sect. 4.5.1).

OER, empowered by online learning technologies such as LMS and mobile technology, catalysed a new flexible path for teacher professional development, i.e., alternative credentials such as micro-credentials. Micro-credentialing represents a recent global endeavour to recognize informal learning, microlearning and nanolearning by lifelong learners. It has also been adopted in teacher professional development in recent years as an effective way to encourage, energize and certify teachers' self-directed learning and micro-learning. It supplements the seat-time and workshop approach to formal teacher professional development programs and particularly suits competence-based learning and skill training. For TVET to stay relevance, micro certification and credentialing systems should be based on agreed industry standards and the identified needs of both learners and employers (Milio et al., 2014; World Economic Forum, 2017). A more in-depth discussion is contained in Sect. 2.2.4).

Professional learning communities (PLC) and communities of practice (CoP) present another flexible venue for TVET Teachers' lifelong professional growth. These two terms are often used interchangeably to refer to a group of professionals sharing their knowledge, skills and practices to develop professionally together. To some scholars such as Blankenship and Ruona (2007), and Beni et al. (2021), PLC is different from CoP in that the former is more compulsory in nature with the involvement of institutional guidance and leadership, while the latter is more grassroot-participatory and less organized, emphasizing the input from community members. Despite the differences, their constructive impacts on fostering lifelong learning and continued professional growth for teachers have been confirmed and acknowledged (see Kong, 2018; Pedersen, 2017; also see Sect. 4.5.2 for more discussion on learning communities).

Modes of Teacher Professional Development

In terms of modes of learning and training, an outstanding feature of teacher professional development in the digital age is the exploitation of a diverse range of technology to support and enable teacher professional learning efforts and opportunities. Humans and machines have never been working so closely together in a partnership, collaborating and interacting with each other. For example, a PLC or CoP can engage teachers in a face-to-face mode or virtually through synchronous/unsynchronous online platforms (e.g., blogs, LMS, Zoom), virtual reality or social media (e.g., Facebook, WeChat and WhatsApp).

In addition, the use of AI and computer algorithms in teacher professional development has received increasing attention in recent years. These technologies are qualitatively transforming the way teacher professional development is conducted, making it more dynamic, adaptive and targeted in learning and more accurate and timely in learning evaluation. Today's AI can identify teachers' needs and intelligently feed on-demand, tailor-made training resources into professional learning and training. As the whole learning process can be recorded, an ongoing multivariate analysis of the teachers' learning data can be timely performed to inform the progress and effectiveness of teacher professional learning and how each individual performs in their learning trajectory.

Shiohira (2021) argues for an immediate and multidimensional engagement with AI by educational and training institutions so as to "promptly respond to both job-specific skills and the transversal skills required to navigate new ways of working and to the renewed requirement for lifelong learning and continuous upskilling" (p. 47). In the same vein, the *Implementation Plan for Training Proficient Teachers (2.0)* issued by Ministry of Education of China (2019a) promotes a seamlessly integration of digital technology into teacher training and professional development. It specifically emphasizes the need for developing a range of interactive and context-specific teacher training resources through the use of technologies such as AI, SMART learning environments, virtual reality, augmented reality and mixed reality.

Indeed, technology has transformed TVET and presented changing challenges and opportunities unique to students and teachers in TVET. The new challenges and opportunities mean more than just upskilling and reskilling in order to survive. They implore educators to reorientate teaching and learning to respond to economic, societal and environmental demands facing the post pandemic workplace globally. More than ever, a new mindset empowered by forward thinking is needed. This rethinking not only prepares TVET students and teachers for the uncertainty brought about by the increasingly digitalized world of work, but also ready themselves for taking better advantage of the opportunities afforded by emerging technologies such as AI), automation and the fifth generation of mobile communication technology (5G). The transformation of TVET is largely hinged on the quality of teachers. Needless to say, holistic, ongoing, flexible and sustainable professional development supported by technology is urgently needed for TVET teachers to stay abreast with the digital transformation of our societies. Such a need became the grounds of this Handbook.

1.5 The Purpose and Scope of the Handbook

This Handbook was the result of the concerted efforts from the International Centre for Higher Education Innovation under the auspices of UNSCO and experts from higher education in China and around the world. Covering both theories and practices in TVET teacher development, this Handbook aims to provide an up-to-date discussion and recommendations on issues relating to TVET teacher competency development and assessment in the digital age. It caters for the needs of in-service teachers and trainers as well as TVET leaders who want to upscale their professional learning and development in terms of vision, knowledge, expertise, and industry skills needed in the transition to the digital world of work. What should be particularly useful to TVET teachers/trainers are the proposed competency development framework, competency indicators, and assessment instrument. Drawing on extensive research on TVET teachers' competency development and today's industry needs, the proposed framework, indicators assessment tool can be readily used by TVET institutions and training organizations to inform the effectiveness of existing teacher training and professional development programs. They can also be used as a self-evaluation tool for individual teachers to assess their professional competency levels so as to plan and adjust one's career trajectory accordingly. Teachers and trainers may also find the exemplary cases of teachers' professional development from various countries inspiring and motivating. The Handbook can also serve as a useful reference for developing professional development policies and programs by TVET leaders, administrators, teachers, and trainers who may find the competency framework, indicators and strategies thought-provoking and adaptable.

This handbook is organized across five chapters, with each chapter consisting of several sections. This chapter provides the background for this research. By situating TVET teacher professional development in the context of digital transformation in education and the Industry 4.0 age, this chapter first discusses digital transformation in TVET and professional competencies needed by TVET teachers to stay relevant in the digital age. It then proceeds to identify the need, resources, strategies and modes for continuing, flexible and sustainable TVET teacher professional development. The second half of this chapter explains the purposes and scope of the Handbook and how it should be used by different readers. Chapter 2 exposits key theories relating to TVET and TVET teacher professional development with a focus on teacher professional development theories needed for the transition to digital TVET. Chapter 3 sees the application of relevant theories to the proposal of a TVET teacher competency framework that categorizes core competencies required of in-service TVET teachers and trainers in different stages of their career trajectory in the digital age. This framework is further developed and substantiated by our proposal of competency indicators and an instrument for evaluating TVET teachers' competencies. Chapter 3 concludes with recommendations for use of the proposed framework, indicators and assessment instrument by different stakeholders at the national, institutional, and individual levels. With a focus on strategies for TVET teachers' professional development, Chapter 4 first proposes an ecological approach that sees teacher professional development as an interaction between different levels of efforts (i.e., national/international, institutional and individual). This is followed by the proposal of a teacher professional development model and a review of the strategies, approaches and resources used to support TVET teachers' professional growth throughout the world. Chapter 5 presents a collection of exemplary cases of teachers' professional development in TVET around the world.

1.6 How to Use This Handbook

This handbook provides resources and references that can be easily used or adapted by in-service TVET teachers as well as administrators and policy makers in their attempt to engage and support effective teacher professional development in a time of digital transformation. This Handbook can be used together with the other two books in this series: (1) the *Handbook of Teaching Competencies Development in Higher Education,* and (2) the *Handbook of Educational Reform through Blended Learning.*

References

Ali, D., & Abdulkadir, D. (2017). Integration of vocational schools to industry 4.0 by updating curriculum and programs. *International Journal of Multidisciplinary Studies and Innovative Technologies, 1*(1), 1–3.

Bai, C., Dallasega, P., Orzes, G., & Sarkis, J. (2020) Industry 4.0 technologies assessment: A sustainability perspective. *International Journal of Production Economics, 229.*

Beni, S., Fletcher, T., & Ni Chróinín, D. (2021). Teachers' engagement with professional development to support implementation of meaningful physical education. *Journal of Teaching in Physical Education.*

Blankenship, S. S., & Ruona, E. A. W. (2007). *Professional learning communities and communities of practice: A comparison of models, literature review.* Paper presented at the Academy of Human Resource Development International Research Conference in the Americas, Indianapolis, IN.

Bossu, C., & Willems, J. (2017). Capacity building for equity and access using open education resources (OER). In H. Partridge, K. Davis, & J. Thomas. (Eds.), *Me, Us, IT! Proceedings ASCILITE2017: 34th international conference on innovation, practice and research in the use of educational technologies in tertiary education* (pp. 22–26).

CEDEFOP. (2015). Stronger VET for better lives: CEDEFOP's monitoring report on vocational education and training policies, 2010–14.

CEDEFOP. (2019). Sharing knowledge for VET future quality: Community scope and achievements. In *CEDEFOP, Thessaloniki, Greece*

China G20. (2014). *Employment plan 2014*. Retrieved August 3, 2022, from http://www.g20.org.tr/wp-content/uploads/2014/12/g20_employment_plan_china.pdf

Diao, J., & Yang, J. (2021). Multiple-role perspective on assessing teaching ability: Reframing TVET teachers' competency in the information age. *Journal of Educational Technology Development and Exchange, 14*(1), 57–77.

Diep, P., & Hartmann, M. (2016). Green skills in vocational teacher education—A model of pedagogical competence for a world of sustainable development. *TVET@Asia, 6,* 1–19.

Han, X., & Wang, Y. (2021). System-driven blended learning for quality education: A collective case study of universities and vocational colleges and schools in China. In C. P. Lim & C. R. Graham (Eds.), *Blended learning for quality access in Asian universities* (pp. 1–23). Springer.

ILO. (2019). *ILO centenary declaration for the future of work*. Adopted by the International Labour Conference, Geneva, Switzerland. https://www.ilo.org/wcmsp5/groups/public/---ed_norm/---relconf/documents/meetingdocument/wcms_711674.pdf. Accessed June 21, 2019.

Jafar, D., Saud, M., Hamid, M., Suhairom, N., Mohd, H., Mohd, H., & Zaid, Y. (2020). TVET teacher professional competency framework in Industry 4.0 era. *Universal Journal of Educational Research, 8,* 1969–1979.

Johnson, J., Loyalka, P., Chu, J., Song, Y., Yi, H., & Huang, X. (2016). The impact of vocational teachers on student learning in developing countries. *Comparative Education Review, 60*(1), 131–150. The University of Chicago Press.

Kong, S. (2018). Community of practice: An effective way to ESL teacher professional development in vocational colleges. *English Language Teaching, 11*(7), 158–162.

Latchem, C. (2017). *Using ICTs and blended learning in transforming TVET.* Available at: https://unevoc.unesco.org/home/UNESCO%20and%20COL%20Publication%20on%20ICTs%20and%20Blended%20Learning. Accessed August 27, 2020.

MacDougall, W. (2014). *Industrie 4.0 Smart manufacturing for the future*. Germans Trade & Investment.

Madsen, E. S., Bilberg, A., & Grube Hansen, D. (2016). Industry 4.0 and digitalization call for vocational skills, applied industrial engineering, and less for pure academics. In *Proceedings of the 5th P&OM world conference P&OM.*

Milio, S., Garnizova, E., & Shkreli, A. (2014). Assessment study of technical and vocational education and training (TVET) in Myanmar. *ILO Asia-Pacific Working Paper Series,* 1–210.

Ministry of Education of China. (2019a). *Implementation plan for training proficient teachers (2.0)*. Retrieved August 3, 2022, from http://www.moe.gov.cn/jyb_xwfb/s5147/201904/t20190403_376571.html

Ministry of Education of China. (2019b). *The implementation plan for further developing TVET teachers' dual roles in the new age*. Retrieved August 3, 2022, from http://www.moe.gov.cn/srcsite/A10/s7034/201910/t20191016_403867.html

Ministry of Education of China. (2022a). *Notice regarding the promotion of TVET teachers' professional competence*. Retrieved August 3, 2022, from http://www.moe.gov.cn/srcsite/A10/s7034/202205/t20220523_629603.html

Ministry of Education of China. (2022b). *The modern vocational education system with Chinese characteristics has been promoted in depth*. Retrieved June 5, 2022 from http://www.moe.gov.cn/fbh/live/2022/54487/sfcl/202205/t20220524_629748.html

Open Educational Resources. (n.d.). Retrieved August 7, 2022 from https://www.unesco.org/en/communication-information/open-solutions/open-educational-resources

Ossiannilsson, E. (2019). OER and OEP for access, equity, equality, quality, inclusiveness, and empowering lifelong learning. *International Journal of Open Educational Resources, 1*(2). Spring/Summer 2019.

Pedersen, K. W. (2017). Supporting collaborative and continuing professional development in education for sustainability through a communities of practice approach. *International Journal of Sustainability in Higher Education, 18*(5), 681–696. ©Emerald Publishing Limited, 1467–6370. https://doi.org/10.1108/IJSHE-02-2016-0033

Philbeck, T., Davis, N. (2018). The fourth industrial revolution. *Journal of International Affairs, 72*(1), 17–22. ISSN 0022-197X. JSTOR 26588339

Schwab, K. (2016). *The fourth industrial revolution: What it means, how to respond*. Foreign Affairs, 12 December 2015

Shiohira, K. (2021). *Understanding the impact of artificial intelligence on skills development*. UNESCO-UNEVOC, Paris, France and Bonn, Germany, 2021. https://unevoc.unesco.org/home/UNEVOC+Publications/lang=en/akt=detail/qs=6448

Sommer, H., & Kreibich, L. (2017). TVET today. In *4th industrial revolution tomorrow possible implications for TVET and The labour market in Vietnam*. Deutsche Gesellschaftfür Internationale Zusammenarbeit (GIZ).

State Council of China. (2019). *The national implementation plan for the reform of vocational education*. Retrieved August 3, 2022, from http://www.gov.cn/zhengce/content/2019-02/13/content_5365341.htm

UNESCO. (2016). *Recommendation concerning technical and vocational education and training (TVET)*.

UNESCO. (2019). *Beijing consensus on artificial intelligence and education*. UNESCO, Paris. https://unesdoc.unesco.org/ark:/48223/pf0000368303

UNESCO (2022). UNESCO TVET Strategy for 2022–2029. From: https://www.unesco.org/en/articles/unesco-launches-new-strategy-tvet-2022-2029-international-conference. Accessed January 10, 2023.

UNESCO-UNEVOC. (2020). *UNESCO-UNEVOC study on the trends shaping the future of TVET teaching*. UNEVOC International Centre for Technical and Vocational Education and Training, Bonn, Germany. Available at: https://unevoc.unesco.org/go.php?q=UNEVOC+Resources+-+Video. Accessed April 17, 2022

UNESCO-UNEVOC. (2022a). *Quality TVET for all*. UNESCO UNEVOC, BONN Germany. Available at: https://unevoc.unesco.org/home/UNESCO-UNEVOC+-+Who+we+are. Accessed April 17, 2022.

UNESCO-UNEVOC. (2022b). *TVET Leadership Programme boosts skills for the digital transformation*. UNESCO UNEVOC, BONN Germany. Available at: https://unevoc.unesco.org/home/TVET+Leadership+Programme+boosts+skills+for+the+digital+transformation. Accessed April 17, 2022.

Wagiran, W., Pardjono, P., Suyanto, W., Sofyan, H., Soenarto, S., & Yudantoko, A. (2019). Competencies of future vocational teachers: Perspective of in-service teachers and educational experts. *Journal Cakrawala Pendidikan, 38*(2), 387–397.

Wang, Y., & Han, X. (2017). Institutional roles in blended learning implementation: A case study of vocational education in China. *International Journal of Technology in Teaching and Learning, 13*(1), 16–32.

Wiley, D., Iii, Hilton, J. L. (2018). Defining OER-enabled pedagogy. *The International Review of Research in Open and Distributed Learning, 19*(4). https://doi.org/10.19173/irrodl.v19i4.3601. ISSN 1492-3831. S2CID 158674318.

World Economic Forum. (2017). Realizing human potential in the fourth industrial revolution an agenda for leaders to shape the future of education, gender and work (pp. 1–35). Switzerland.

Yu, C., Xu, X., & Lu, Y. (2015). Computer-integrated manufacturing, cyber-physical systems and cloud manufacturing—concepts and relationships. *Manufacturing Letters, 6*, 5–9.

Zaharah, S., Selamat, M.N., Alavi, K., & Arifin, K. (2018). Industry 4.0: A systematic review in technical and vocational education and training. *Jurnal Psikologi Malaysia, 32*(4), 66–74. ISSN-2289-8174

Open Access This chapter is licensed under the terms of the Creative Commons Attribution-NonCommercial-NoDerivatives 4.0 International License (http://creativecommons.org/licenses/by-nc-nd/4.0/), which permits any noncommercial use, sharing, distribution and reproduction in any medium or format, as long as you give appropriate credit to the original author(s) and the source, provide a link to the Creative Commons license and indicate if you modified the licensed material. You do not have permission under this license to share adapted material derived from this chapter or parts of it.

The images or other third party material in this chapter are included in the chapter's Creative Commons license, unless indicated otherwise in a credit line to the material. If material is not included in the chapter's Creative Commons license and your intended use is not permitted by statutory regulation or exceeds the permitted use, you will need to obtain permission directly from the copyright holder.

Chapter 2
Definitions and a Review of Relevant Theories, Frameworks, and Approaches

Jihua Song, Zhixian Zhong, Chun He, Hongyan Lu, Xibin Han, Xibei Xiong, and Yuping Wang

2.1 Introduction

This chapter focuses on a review of the literature on the theories, frameworks, and approaches that inform teacher professional development in vocational education. We first define the scope of vocational education and teacher professional competencies in this introduction. This is followed by an exposition of theories, frameworks, and approaches on teacher professional competency development that contribute to teacher professional development in vocational education.

2.1.1 Defining the Scope of Vocational Education

There has been a proliferation of terms used to refer to vocational education. According to Ouyang (2003), there are over 30 terms describing vocational education. They include Apprenticeship Training, Vocational Education, Technical Vocational Education (TVE), Occupational Education (OE), Vocational Education and Training

---

J. Song (✉) · C. He
School of Artificial Intelligence, Beijing Normal University, Beijing, China
e-mail: sjh13@163.com

Z. Zhong · H. Lu
Institute of Teacher Education for Advanced Study, Jiangxi Normal University, Nanchang, China

X. Han
Institute of Education, Tsinghua University, Beijing, China

X. Xiong
School of Education, Guangxi Normal University, Guilin, China

Y. Wang
School of Humanities, Languages and Social Science, Griffith University, Brisbane, Australia

© The Author(s) 2024
X. Han et al. (eds.), *Handbook of Technical and Vocational Teacher Professional Development in the Digital Age*, SpringerBriefs in Education,
https://doi.org/10.1007/978-981-99-5937-2_2

(VET), Career and Technical Education (CTE), Workforce Education (WE), Workplace Education (WE), among others. Since 1999, the term of Technological and Vocational Education and Training (TVET) has replaced most of the other terms to because the "official" vernacular used in academic publications and official documents, particularly in UNESCO documents and policy statements. TVET was first adopted at the Second International Conference on Vocational Education held in Seoul, capital of South Korea in April 1999. This is the term used in this Handbook.

How should we define TVET? UNESCO-UNEVOC defines TVET as "comprising education, training and skills development relating to a wide range of occupational fields, production, services and livelihoods," "as part of lifelong learning," and that it "can take place at secondary, post-secondary and tertiary levels and includes work-based learning and continuing training and professional development which may lead to qualifications". UNESCO-UNEVOC further points out that TVET helps learners to develop a wide range of skills such as learning to learn, "literacy and numeracy skills, transversal skills and citizenship skills" (https://unevoc.unesco.org/home/TVETipedia+Glossary/filt). This handbook adopts the above definition of TVET as our basic understanding when discussing issues in TVET.

TVET has been regarded as an important venue for achieving social equity, inclusion and sustainable development by UNESCO (https://unevoc.unesco.org/home/fwd2UNESCO-UNEVOC+-+Who+We+Are). In 2019, China released "The Implementation Plan for National Vocational Education Reform," which promoted the importance of TVET by stating that "vocational education and general education are two different types of education with equal importance".

2.1.2 Defining the Basic Tenets in TVET Teachers' Professional Competencies

TVET teachers' professional development has never been so crucial as it is today when rapid changes in education and industry are transforming TVET in every possible way. TVET teachers must develop and upgrade their professional knowledge, teaching competencies, and innovative teaching strategies to meet the diverse and personalized educational requirements of industry and learners (Guthrie, 2010). This is a lifelong journey that requires the concerted efforts from both teachers as individuals and from governments and institutions. UNESCO and other relevant international organizations such as UNEVOC have played a major role in TVET teachers' development throughout the world. As promoted in "the UNESCO TVET Strategy 2016–2021," competent TVET teachers are essential for the quality and development of TVET, because they are the key agent for equipping future workforce with knowledge, skills, and disposition to meet the needs of a rapidly changing labor market, and contribute to the sustainable development of the society.

What professional competencies are required of today's TVET teachers? Before we discuss teacher competencies, we need to define what competency entails in this study to lay a foundation for building our understanding of teacher competencies. The definition we adopted here reflects the established arguments in the literature. That is, a competency refers to the combination of one's knowledge, skills, and personal attributes such as attitudes, disposition, beliefs, and values that makes one professionally competent (Koster & Dengerink, 2008; Rychen & Salganik, 2003). In this handbook, we also use the word 'competence' in a broader and more general sense to refer to one's ability in accomplishing something.

In this handbook, we make a clear distinction between teaching competencies and professional competencies in that the former focuses on pedagogical capacities of a teacher such as knowledge and pedagogical skills while the latter involves other attributes as a teacher such as attitudes, beliefs, and dispositions, in addition to teaching competencies. In other words, teacher professional competencies are more inclusive than teaching competencies. We also stress that the requirements for teacher professional competencies have never ceased to evolve and expand over time. This capacities approach to the understanding of teachers' competence is largely in line with the dominant views in scholarly debates about basic capacity requirements for teachers (Feiman-Nemser, 2001; Grant, 2008; Williamson McDiarmid & Clevenger-Bright, 2008). There is a substantial body of literature on teacher capacities and competencies in general education (see a review by Caena, 2011). In her comprehensive review of the literature on approaches and debates regarding the definitions of teacher competence, Caena (2011) synthesized the key elements of teacher competence requirements as follows. In terms of the requirements of knowledge, the following areas were identified:

- subject matter knowledge
- pedagogical subject knowledge
- pedagogical knowledge
- curricular knowledge
- educational sciences foundations (intercultural, historical, philosophical, psychological, sociological knowledge)
- contextual, institutional, organizational aspects of educational policies
- issues of inclusion and diversity
- new technologies
- developmental psychology
- group processes and dynamics, learning theories, motivational issues
- evaluation and assessment processes and methods (p. 28).

—In terms of skills, a teacher should possess:

- planning, managing, and coordinating teaching
- using teaching materials and technologies
- managing students and groups
- monitoring and assessing learning
- collaborating with colleagues, parents and social services
- negotiating skills

- collaborative, reflective, and interpersonal skills for learning in professional communities
- ability to adapt to multi-level dynamics with cross-influences (from government policies to student, classroom and school dynamics)
- ability to draw conclusions and decisions on the basis of interpretations of evidence and data, for teaching and learning enhancement (p. 28).

—In terms of values, the following were identified:

- epistemological awareness (i.e., about relevant issues of the features and historical development of the subject area and its status, as related to other subject areas)
- dispositions to change
- commitment to promoting the learning of all students
- dispositions to promote students' democratic attitudes and practices, as future European citizens
- dispositions to flexibility and ongoing learning
- dispositions to examining, discussing, questioning one's own practices (p. 28).

We recognize that teacher competencies are complex, multifaceted, and evolving with time, and that the above lists are not exhaustive. However, they can be used as a checklist when discussing teachers' competency standards and requirements. Although these elements were gleaned from the literature relating to general education, they are readily applicable to TVET. We also noted that transformative changes in education and our society have occurred in the last decade since Caena's (2011) review was conducted and that teacher competencies should be revisited and updated accordingly. This is especially true with teachers' ICT competencies as we enter the digital era. In TVET, developing teachers' ICT competence is not an option, but a must due to the digital transformation happening on campus and in industry. For both teachers and learners, existing knowledge and skills need to be upgraded and new skills need to be developed to meet the changing demands from workplace and personal growth. In view of such needs, many scholars and practitioners in TVET have proposed new competencies required of TVET teachers today. For example, Han et al. (2019) suggested that core ICT competencies for TVET teachers can consist of seven dimensions: awareness, attitude, knowledge, skills, learning design and development, implementation, and evaluation. To Zhang and Rong (2011), TVET teachers should be competent in the following six aspects as far as ICT supported learning is concerned: understanding ICT supported/enabled learning, curriculum and assessment development, pedagogical proficiency, proficient use of ICT and technological equipment, ability to create ICT-supported learning environments, and ability to self-develop with the support of ICT. A more detailed discussion on TVET teachers' digital teaching competencies is contained in the next chapter.

2.2 Frameworks and Approaches Adopted in TVET Teachers' Professional Competency Development

This section briefly reviews some key frameworks and approaches that have been adopted in TVET teachers' professional development. Empirical studies implementing and evaluating these frameworks and approaches are also reviewed for a better understanding of these frameworks and approaches.

2.2.1 The TPACK Framework

As a framework that describes the professional knowledge needed for teaching with technology, TPACK (Technological pedagogical content knowledge) was introduced by Koehler and Mishra (2005). The three core components of knowledge in the TPACK framework are content knowledge (CK), pedagogical knowledge (PK), and technological knowledge (TK). The other components of pedagogical and content knowledge (PCK), technological content knowledge (TCK), and technological pedagogical knowledge (TPK) in TPACK are knowledge developed through the interactions between and among these bodies of core knowledge mediated by the use of technology (Koehler & Mishra, 2009). In the words of Cox and Graham (2009), TPACK is "teacher's knowledge of how to coordinate subject-or topic-specific activities with topic-specific representations using emerging technologies to facilitate student learning" (p. 64).

There is a large number of studies that have employed TPACK to investigate vocational education teachers' competencies and documented empirical evidence for an in-depth understanding of vocational education teachers' competencies. For example, Miao et al. (2016) surveyed 140 teachers from 13 vocational colleges in Chongqing, China, in regard to teachers' perceived TPACK competencies. Their findings revealed that there was a tendency of overfocusing on the development of technological knowledge at the expense of the development of pedagogical and content knowledge. Therefore, they proposed that the professional development for TVET teachers should attach greater importance to pedagogical and content knowledge when integrating technological knowledge into teaching. Guided by the TPACK framework, Ran and Cai (2017) investigated the level of TPACK competencies of teachers who were both teachers and trainers in secondary vocational colleges in China. In view of the many challenges facing these teachers, they recommended to establish an in-company teacher training system, build learning communities, develop ICT competencies for instructional design and delivery, and implement professional development programs at different levels.

In recent years, the TPACK framework has undergone some updating and restructuring to reflect the changes and new demands in education, particularly those brought about by digital transformation. Adopting an andragogical approach, Arifin et al., (2020) revised the TPACK framework and proposed a new acronym "TAWOCK" to denote a Technology Andragogy Work Content Knowledge Model. This model was developed specifically for TVET. It is characterized by a learner-centered approach and takes workplace learning and training into consideration. Our literature review indicates that it is still a conceptual model at this stage in need of empirical validation. Another adaption of the TPACK framework to the TVET context was proposed by Tang and Bai (2021). With a strong emphasis on TVET related content, knowledge, and technological-pedagogical proficiency, this model aims to further our understanding of TVET teachers' competency requirements in the 5G era. There are four parts in this adapted framework: V-TK (vocational technological knowledge), V-TCK (vocational technological and content knowledge), V-TPK (vocational technological and pedagogical knowledge), and V-TPACK.

2.2.2 The COMET Model

COMET stands for "Competence Development and Assessment in TVET." This is a competence diagnostics model that was specifically developed for TVET. It takes into consideration the special features, or the diverse and complex requirements and demands of TVET, in terms of competence development and assessment in both the classroom and workplace. Originated in Germany in 2006 and led by Professor Felix Rauner, the COMET project has now been developed into an international research consortium participated by countries such as China and South Africa (Rauner et al., 2013a, 2013b). As commented by Lahn and Nore (2019) (Zhao & Rauner, 2020), the primary goal of this project was to establish a theoretical and methodological system to support the pedagogical work of TVET teachers. A secondary aim was to construct a benchmark for international comparisons that will inform policymaking and education reform in TVET. Rauner (2021) mentioned, "In less than a decade, the methods of competence diagnostics in accordance with the COMET test procedure have become an internationally established instrument for quality assurance and quality development in vocational education and training" (p. v).

Briefly, the COMET model, in some ways, can be regarded as the TVET equivalent of PISA (The Program for International Student Assessment). It offers a large-scale competence diagnostics method for quantitative evaluations of the advancement of students' occupational competencies, career commitments, and professional identity. There are three interconnected dimensions in this model: the requirement dimension (competence levels including shaping competence, processual, functional, and nominal competence), the content dimension, referring to areas of learning at different levels (beginning, advanced, professional and expert), and the action dimension progressing from informing, planning, deciding, conducting, controlling to assessing). For a diagram of this model, see Rauner et al., (2013b), p. 42. Each dimension has its own theoretical and normative bases. Competence measurement instruments and test tasks based on COMET were also developed and evaluated by TVET researchers and practitioners around the world. Rauner (2021) provided a method manual book providing a detailed and updated discussion of this model and the relevant instruments for competence measurement developed since the inception of this model. One can also find empirical studies adopting this model and these test instruments in this book.

The COMET model was also adapted to teacher professional development in TVET to develop a TPD (Teachers of Professional Disciplines) competence and measurement model for TVET teachers. Its validity was confirmed by empirical studies such as the one reported in Zhao and Zhuang (2012). Their study largely confirmed the validity of the test tasks and the competence model.

2.2.3 The SMART Framework for Teacher Professional Development

In the last 10 years, terminologies such as smart learning, smart education, and smart learning environment have been frequently used by researchers exploring the affordances of ICT in supporting or enabling learning. While the lack of consensus on the definition of smart education is recognized in the literature (Hoel & Mason, 2018; Zhu et al., 2016), there have been many attempts to explore its theoretical basis, characteristics, and practical implications. The following defining features of smart education can be gleaned from the literature. Smart education involves, but is not limited to:

- the creation of intelligent environments by using smart technologies and the adoption of smart pedagogies that facilitate personalized learning and empower learners to develop wisdom (Zhu & Bin, 2012).
- a smart learning environment that is "effective, efficient and engaging" (Spector, 2014, p. 2).
- a better and faster learning enriched by digital, context-aware and adaptive devices (Koper, 2014, p. 1).

The smart education concept has also been adopted in teacher professional development to meet the needs of teachers in a time of digital transformation. For example, Zhong (2020a, 2020b) investigated teacher development from the perspective of SMART education and proposed a SMART education framework to guide the professional development of teachers. The central tenet of this framework regards today's teachers as smart teachers empowered by technology. This framework is composed of five interrelated constructs represented by S, M, A, R and T. S represents SMART-education directed; M refers to Self-managed; A is Adaptive; R stands for Reflective; and T means Technology-empowered.

SMART Education Idea Directed

Applying the concept of smart education to teachers' professional development, this framework places a strong emphasis on advancing teachers capacities in fostering students' abilities and skills in critical thinking, innovation, collaboration, communication, and problem solving. SMART education also requires teachers to develop digital competence to innovate teaching and improve student learning. Finally, SMART education also means the adoption of innovative evaluation models, and making evaluation more automated, intelligent, and personalized (Gu et al., 2021).

Self-Managed

Self-management is a crucial strategy for teachers' lifelong development. The lifelong and continuing professional development of a teacher is essentially a process and result of self-management (Zhong, 2008). Self-management refers to the effective control and adjustment of self-awareness, emotion, and behavior on the basis of fully understanding how to achieve the goal. It is the active and effective monitoring and adjustment from self-awareness to behavior. The core of self-management is self-regulation, or the ability to actively participate in and be responsible for one's own activities, including strategies, self-efficacy, self-efforts, and self-reflection. Self-management can be categorized into the following 10 focal areas: basic knowledge, self-awareness, goal management, resource management, time management, pressure management, emotion management, effort management, interpersonal relation management, and self-evaluation management (Zhong, 2015).

Adaptive

In the digital age, being adaptive should be a learning mode by default. As far as teachers' professional growth is concerned, being adaptive means to have the ability to change in order to meet the demands of digital transformation. Thus, a SMART teacher needs to develop adaptability in the following four aspects:

- Being self-driven: Teachers should be the active agent driving their self-development and lifelong learning. They should develop a sense of ownership of their learning and manage their professional development with a degree of independence and sovereignty.
- Being smart in ICT-supported professional development: Teachers should develop the ability to use ICT and digital resources smartly to suit their own individual needs and support their professional development.
- Personalizing learning in professional development: In the digital age, teachers' professional development should identify individual differences and cater for individual growth through more targeted and customized learning design, teamwork,

and role play. With the support of adaptive technology such an approach can maximize the potential of individual teachers.
- DIY learning: DIY learning refers to self-organized learning often occurring at workplace. It is self-initiated, often an informal, lifelong learning empowered by technology and sustained by one's adaptivity. DIY learning allows teachers to design and develop their own professional trajectory.

Reflective

This construct refers to teachers' growth through reflection. Reflection is widely regarded as a determining factor in teachers' professional development. Without reflection, there would be no continuous professional growth of teachers (Calderhead & Gates, 2003). Teachers' reflection is the process in which teachers constantly improve their educational and teaching efficiency and student learning outcomes by reflecting on their teaching experiences and analyzing and correcting their own behaviors in teaching practice. The process features reflection on the practicality, pertinence, time-efficiency, self-examination, and procedure of their teaching process (Zhang, 2001). Metacognition and meta-learning are the core competencies of teachers' reflective growth. Meta-cognition is a process of reflection, which involves reflection on one's own current situation, future goals, potential behaviors and strategies, and expected outcomes. Meta-learning is closely related to metacognition. What is more important to teacher development is meta-learning that cultivates a growth mindset and a firm belief in change and development. It recognizes the importance of the intrinsic motivation of teachers in their continuous growth and development (Fadel et al., 2015). Teachers' metacognition and meta-learning are premised on reflection, which in turn promotes teachers' professional growth.

Technology-Empowered

Technology has empowered every aspect of education, creating a new ecology in education. SMART teachers must also be empowered by technology. Technological empowerment embraces both the enabling and augmenting power of technology. The former makes what is impossible possible and the latter makes what is powerful more powerful (Zhu & Peng, 2021). In this process, it is important to be rational. For instance, allowing machines do what is suitable for machines, people do what is suitable for people, and people and machines do what is suitable for human–machine cooperation (Zhu & Wei, 2018). Technologies and teachers will become a community to undertake educational tasks (Zhong, 2020a, 2020b).

2.2.4 Micro-credentialing

Micro-credentialing is a direct response to the demands for recognizing one's constant efforts in upgrading knowledge and skills needed by today's digitalized society. Together with other credentials such as digital badges and industry-recognized certificates, micro-credentials form part of the so-called alternative credentials that are gaining interest among learners from all walks of life in the last decades (Kato et al., 2020; OECD, 2021). European Commission (2020) defined micro-credentials as a "proof of the learning outcomes that a learner has acquired following a short learning experience." and the acquired learning outcomes have been "assessed against transparent standards" (p. 10). According to Berry and Cator (2016), micro-credentials were competency-based, personalized, on-demand and shareable. They are also research-backed (https://digitalpromise.org/initiative/educator-micro-credentials/). OECD (2021) summarized 12 desirable characteristics of micro-credentials:

> targeted (breath), rapid (duration), flexible (sequencing or timing), stackable (with institution), learning outcomes assessed (using sectoral or national assessment framework), external assurance of program or provider, portable (applicable to study programs in other higher education institutions), study load expressed in credits, located with National Qualification Framework, employer role in credential design/approval, wage or occupation reporting and self-sovereign digital identity (recipient ownership, vendor independence). (p. 4)

Micro-credentialing, empowered by online learning resources, Open Educational Resources (OERs) and emerging technologies such as online platforms and social media, offers a flexible way to personalize one's micro unit learning and lifelong learning. It offers a new pathway for learners to receive formal recognition for learning of this kind, supplementing what formal educational programs lacks, in terms of flexibility. Micro-credential programs have been offered in schools, higher education (at both undergraduate and postgraduate levels), vocational education, and industry throughout the world. Their effectiveness has generally been recognized and confirmed (for a more detailed discussion on micro-credentials see OECD, 2021). In TVET, the importance of micro-credentials is highlighted for meeting the needs of the post pandemic workplace. As such, micro-credentials have been suggested to be extended to micro-apprenticeships (Seet & Jones, 2021).

Micro-credentials have also been adopted in teacher professional development in recent years. In view of the inefficiency of seat-time and workshop approach to formal teacher professional development programs and in recognition of teachers' informal self-development efforts, many educational institutions around the world offer micro-credentials to their staff as a certification of skill development (OECD, 2021). For example, Digital Promise, a US non-profit organization, launched the first micro-credentials for K12 educators in the US in 2014. To date, it has partnered with over 50 organizations in the US to develop an ecosystem promoting micro-credentials to higher education institutions, schools, and other organizations (https://digitalpromise.org/initiative/educator-micro-credentials/). Micro-credentials meet the needs of the competency-oriented nature of teacher education reform in the US and reflect its outcome-driven approach in teachers' professional development (Wei & Zhu, 2017). Crow (2017) promoted micro credentials as "an emerging learning design that shows promise for offering educators an on-ramp for identifying and meeting classroom-specific professional learning needs" (p. 4).

2.3 Theories Informing TVET Teachers' Professional Development

This section reviews key theories that inform TVET teachers' professional development. When reviewing each theory, we first explain the basic tenets of the theory and the scholarly debates surrounding the theory under discussion. Empirical studies are then cited to demonstrate how it has been applied to practice, with a particular focus on examples of its application in recent TVET teachers' professional development, whenever possible.

2.3.1 Lifelong Learning Theory

The concept of lifelong, originating in the 1970s, had been confined to adult education until 1996 when the Delors Report (UNESCO, 1996) was published. In this report, OECD Education Ministers called for "lifelong learning for all" and adopted it as a framework to guide educational policy making (OECD, 2001). Up to this day, the framework has not only provided a broad basis for us to understand what lifelong learning entails, but also informed research and policy formulation in relation to lifelong learning. Rapid societal and technological changes in the twenty-first century have made lifelong learning part of the education system today. In particular, the launch of Sustainable Development Goal 4 (SDG 4) in 2015 by the United Nations has brought renewed global attention to lifelong learning. SDG 4 calls on Member States to "ensure inclusive and equitable quality education and promote lifelong learning opportunities for all" (https://www.un.org/en/academic-impact/page/sustainable-development-goals). In reviewing research on lifelong learning, the following perspectives have emerged strongly:

- In terms of learning span, lifelong learning covers the whole course of one's life, from cradle to grave (Commission of the European Communities, 2006; OECD, 2001; UNESCO Delors Report, 1996). This definition clearly differentiates lifelong learning from adult learning and further education.
- In terms of mode of learning, "lifelong learning should encompass the whole spectrum of formal, nonformal and informal learning" (Commission of the European Communities, 2006, p. 3).

- In terms of objectives of learning, the four objectives suggested by the Commission of the European Communities (2006) are comprehensive and illuminating. Lifelong learning aims to develop and promote *active citizenship, personal fulfilment, social inclusion, and employment-related advancements.*
- In terms of learning approaches, self-directed learning, autonomous learning, and self-determined leaning are some of the key approaches that have been widely taken by lifelong learners. The concept of heutagogy has also been advocated as an overarching approach to respond to the needs of lifelong learners (Blaschke, 2012).
- In terms of underpinning principles, lifelong learning is based on four pillars: learning to know, learning to do, learning to live together, and learning to be (UNESCO, 1996). Learner-centeredness, equal opportunities, and the quality and relevance of opportunities are also principles applied to lifelong learning (European Communities, 2006)

Clearly, lifelong learning is important to everyone and has particular and profound implications for teachers and their professional development. These fundamental tenets of lifelong learning have also informed teachers' professional growth as lifelong learners. When discussing teachers as lifelong learners, Zhu (2004) pointed out that the changing demands from today's education made lifelong professional development inevitable if teachers wanted to stay current with the advancements in knowledge and education systems, and if they wanted to be competent and innovative in playing the roles required of them. Furthermore, Tang's (2006) research indicated that transforming teacher education from the one-off model to lifelong education, and eventually, to lifelong learning largely depended on teachers themselves.

Lifelong learning is much more crucial and urgently needed in TVET. This is because the technological transformation happening in TVET education and workplace requires students and teachers to upgrade their knowledge and skills throughout their life. This is why lifelong learning was clearly articulated in a Strategy for TVET (2016–2021). This Strategy promises support for "the efforts of Member States to enhance the relevance of their TVET systems and to equip all youth and adults with the skills required for employment, decent work, entrepreneurship and lifelong learning, and to contribute to the implementation of the 2030 Agenda for Sustainable Development as a whole".

2.3.2 Situated Learning

Situated learning is a learning theory that examines the importance of context and culture to learning. Carr et al. (1998) believed that understanding learning required careful consideration of cultural and situational factors, or the behavior and value orientation in the cultural context. Reviewing the literature on situated learning, Carr et al. (1998) synthesized the key beliefs embraced in this learning theory as follows:

- Knowledge is a product of activity, not a process of acquisition.
- Learning is a process of enculturation in a community of practice (Brown et al., 1989); Communities of practice are discussed in Sect. 2.3.5.
- Learning is developing an identity as a member of a community of practice (Lave & Wenger, 1991).
- Meaning is socially constructed through negotiation.
- Learning in situ engages different socio-cognitive process than learning in schools (p. 6).

Similarly, to Lave and Wenger (1991) "learning is an integral and inseparable aspect of social practice" (p. 31). This perspective led them to coin the concept of legitimate peripheral participation that explains how newcomers become old timers through participation in a community of practice. Another important concept contained in situated learning is cognitive apprenticeship that emphasizes learning through authentic practices and social interaction (Brown et al., 1989). Section 2.3.4 contains a more detailed discussion on cognitive apprenticeship.

Situated learning has long been adopted in teacher training and professional development in both higher and vocational education. Empirical studies have also established its importance in advancing teacher learning and transferring theory into practice in many significant ways. As far as TVET is concerned, a number of learning/training models and theoretical frameworks have been informed by situated learning theories, for example, the workplace learning model proposed by Illeris (2011). Through a comprehensive review of workplace leaning literature, Zhao and Ko (2018) proposed a workplace learning model specially catering for the needs of TVET teachers' continuing professional development. This model recognizes the importance of workplace dynamics in developing TVET teachers' professional identity and competence through situational and practical learning situations. Though still a theoretical framework, the model could be used to facilitate empirical research into TVET professionals' journey to become "double qualified" teachers who possess both pedagogical/academic expertise and technical abilities (Yu, 2015). In a more general context, Chen (2016) believed that integrating situated learning in teacher education can innovate the process of teacher' learning and development. Informed by the situated learning theory, she suggested the following strategies to promote teacher education:

- Transforming teachers' perspectives on learning through providing opportunities for teachers to engage in authentic task completion in collaboration with industry.
- Creating communities of practice for teachers to interact with one another.
- Encouraging teachers to self-manage and self-direct their learning through participation
- Providing a variety of situated learning opportunities to support teacher development.

Xie and Li (2006) believed that practice and situated learning should be an integral part of teacher education. According to them, one of the reasons for ineffective teacher training was lack of real and authentic training environments. With its emphasis on authentic situations and learner participation, situated learning makes teacher training more effective. Zhou (2017) claimed that with the introduction of the concepts promoted in the situated learning theory, such as situated cognition, legitimate peripheral participation, and cognitive apprenticeships, teacher training in China has been transformed from a "delivery—application" model to a "participation—problem solving" model. Close attention has been paid to the intrinsic needs of teachers that focus on constructing learning communities through encouraging teacher participation and other ongoing professional support mechanisms. In such communities teachers developed new skills, shared ideas, and grew into autonomous learners. Meanwhile, with respect to educational practicum and internship, Yang and Chang (2010) promoted the integration of situated learning with pre-service teacher training during their internship. They observed that many pre-service teachers had experienced a reality shock or praxis shock during their internship by failing to apply the theoretical knowledge learned in the classroom to real teaching situations. Situated learning, to some degree, can help reduce this kind of shock.

2.3.3 Adult Learning Theory

Although developed in the 1970s, adult learning theory still remains the cornerstone of the theories and approaches developed and adopted in teacher education and professional development. As its name suggests, adult learning theory is about how adults learn as opposed to how children learn. It is often used interchangeably with andragogy. In his seminal work, Knowles (1978) proposed the following five assumptions about adult learners based on Lindeman's (1926) work: (1) intrinsic motivation is important as they feel the need to learn, (2) learning is self-directed as they need to be responsible for their own learning, (3) learning is facilitated and enriched by experience, (4) learning is practical and relevant to their life and work, and (5) learning focuses on problem solving rather than content learning.

In the last 50 years, this understanding of adult learning and learners has given rise to many instructional strategies for fostering each of these assumptions. At the same time, although these key assumptions remain central to the adult learning theory, theoretical development and educational practices have enriched this theory to a great extent. Indeed, as recognized by Merriam (2008), "there is an ever-expanding understanding of what adult learning is and can be" (p. 98). In discussing what adult learning theory encompasses in the twenty-first century, Merriam (2008) proposed that "that adult learning theory is attending more to the various contexts where learning takes place and to its multidimensional nature" (p. 93). An important development of adult learning theory is transformative learning that emphasizes the transformative power of reflecting on one's existing knowledge and experience (Mezirow, 2000), and making meaning of one's experience (Merriam & Bierema, 2014).

The adult learning theory has been applied to practices in almost every disciplinary area and has a profound impact on teacher education and professional development. Lu (2010) reported his study on the impacts of adult learning theory on teachers' competency development and suggested that teachers, being adult learners, have their unique learning characteristics. Accordingly, teacher training should take into consideration the characteristics and principles of adult learning, and explore an effective participatory training model. When discussing the effective development of TVET teachers' dual role as a teacher and trainer, Peng (2014) proposed a training model that focuses on developing teachers' competencies for problem solving, teaching innovation, and self-development.

In reference to the key concepts in adult learning theory, such as self-directed learning, experiential learning, transformative learning, Pei and Li (2014) advocated the importance of knowing teachers' learning orientation, goals, motivation, and approaches. They believed that teacher development should recognize teachers' self-concept and personal experiences, and stimulate teachers' intrinsic motivation. These can be achieved through placing teacher development in everyday teaching situations, authentic learning environments, and communities of practice (e.g., in schools, communities, or social circles). Such teacher development can facilitate teachers' constant self-transformation that also transforms learners in many ways such as knowledge construction, value systems, and disposition.

2.3.4 Cognitive Apprenticeship

Cognitive apprenticeship was first proposed by Collins et al. (1989). It was based on the notion that apprenticeship showed and guided the apprentice on how to do a task until the apprentice was proficient enough to accomplish the task independently (Collins et al., 1991). However, it differs from the traditional apprenticeship in that cognitive apprenticeship focuses more on raising the learner's awareness of the process of task completion, the contexts of the task, and the wider applicability and transferability of the skills learned. In the words of Collins et al. (1991), in order to translate the model of traditional apprenticeship to cognitive apprenticeship, teachers need to:

- identify the processes of the task and make them visible to students.
- situate abstract tasks in authentic contexts, so that students understand the relevance of the work.
- vary the diversity of situations and articulate the common aspects so that students can transfer what they learn (p. 3).

Collins et al. (1991) further advocated six teaching methods in the context of cognitive apprenticeship. They are modeling, coaching, scaffolding articulation, reflection, and exploration. As Collins et al. explained:

Modeling, coaching, and scaffolding are the core of cognitive apprenticeship, designed to help students acquire an integrated set of skills through processes of observation and guided practice. Articulation and reflection are methods designed to help students both to focus their observations of expert problem solving and to gain conscious access to (and control of) their own problem-solving strategies. Exploration is aimed at encouraging learner autonomy, not only in carrying out expert problem-solving processes but also in defining or formulating the problems to be solved. (p. 13)

Zhong (2008) explained that cognitive apprenticeship addressed the key problems in school education, and integrated the core elements of traditional apprenticeship into school education. Cognitive apprenticeship is premised on the assumption that it facilitates the development of learners' higher-order thinking skills, and in particular, critical thinking skills and complex problem-solving skills. Zhang and Yang (2005) summarized the following features of cognitive apprenticeship as it:

- brings more learners' attention to the process of problem solving, cognitive and meta-cognitive strategies involved in experts' acquisition of knowledge.
- makes what is invisible visible in regard to teachers' or experts' inner cognitive development. Such visibility makes it easier for learners to observe, model and practice.
- situates abstract learning prescribed in the school curriculum in meaningful contexts, and connects learning with workplace environments. This allows learners to fully understand the purpose of learning and how they should apply learning to real tasks. This is also a process of modeling the expert's behaviors.
- encourages learners to reflect on and clearly articulate the shared principles applied to different tasks, so that learners develop the capacity to apply their knowledge and skills independently to new problem-solving situations.
- allows the learner to participate in a variety of cognitive activities during the process of completing complex tasks, and externalizing the complex cognitive process through discussion, role playing, and group problem solving. This process will promote the development of meta-cognitive skills, such as self-correction and self-monitoring.

In recent years, teacher training models have been constructed in accordance with the core concepts in cognitive apprenticeship. For example, Hu (2019) adopted authentic tasks, modeling, workshop, and other important elements from cognitive apprenticeship to build a training model for new teachers. This model allowed new teachers to immerse themselves in real classroom teaching contexts and model expert teachers' behaviors in workshops during the training period. Under the guidance of expert teachers, new teachers gradually developed expertise and tacit knowledge through hands-on learning and real problem solving. This model effectively shortened the time for new teachers to adapt to their new occupations and increased their sense of achievement. Qin and Zeng. (2019) pointed out that cognitive apprenticeship could effectively promote the teaching competencies of young teachers in applied colleges. They also suggested two strategies for developing new teachers' teaching competence: peer mentoring and teamwork. Chen and Zhang (2009) recognized that cognitive apprenticeship required a smaller teacher-student ratio. When class sizes are small, apprenticeship is easier to manage and learning is more effective. In this case, they proposed to take advantage of today's technology to achieve small group learning. ICT could support effective mentor–mentee interaction. The use and design of cognitive apprenticeship in online environments have enriched cognitive apprenticeship.

2.3.5 Community of Practice

The concept and practice of Community of Practice (CoP) is not new and has gained popularity since the 1990s. The rapid ICT advancements have also brought a renewed academic attention to this concept in the last 20 years. ICT has empowered CoP in many important fashions, making it more accessible, sustainable, creative, and productive (Dubé et al., 2005; Kietzmann et al., 2013). CoPs are commonly understood as "groups of people who share a concern, a set of problems, or a passion about a topic, and who deepen their knowledge and expertise in this area by interacting on an ongoing basis" (Wenger et al., 2002, p. 4). In the same vain, Pór (2004) defined CoPs as "self-organizing and self-governing groups of people who share a passion for the common domain of what they do and strive to become better practitioners" (p. 7). Pór also pointed out that together members in CoPs "create value for their members and stakeholders," develop and spread "new knowledge, productive capabilities," (p. 7) and foster innovation.

While Jameson et al. (2006) highlighted the importance of building trust, knowledge sharing, and collaborative leadership in online CoPs, Zhong and Zhu (2011) stressed the participatory nature of CoPs in terms of co-creation of knowledge and community identity. CoPs are sometimes used interchangeably with terminologies such as learning communities and communities of interest. However, "the sentiment of the CoP model as a collaborative learning experience has permeated the breadth of approaches used" (Pedersen, 2017, p. 685).

CoPs have become an established conceptual lens and strategy for teachers' professional development and lifelong learning. Their facilitative quality of fostering continued professional development has been confirmed in terms of collegial support, cross-disciplinary collaborative learning, and sustained professional development efforts (see Kong, 2018; Perdersen, 2017; Sterrett et al., 2015). Cai (2021) discussed the possibilities of building a university—primary–secondary school teachers community, to explore issues such as internal culture-driven mechanisms, trans-disciplinary interaction, collaboration, and structural dynamics of CoPs.

In recent years, a range of technologies, in particular, social media and online platforms, have been adopted in the support of teachers' collaboration and interaction within CoPs. For example, Kong (2018) reported a study on the use of WeChat group as a venue for ESL (English as a Second Language) teachers' professional development in TVET. Findings from this study indicated that WeChat effectively facilitated the communication and interaction among their CoP members.

2.3.6 The Interconnected Model of Professional Growth

The importance of understanding the *process* of teacher professional growth and the interrelated factors that foster the process has long been recognized in research and practice. Models for explaining such a process have been acknowledged and/or explored by a number of research studies (see Cobb et al., 1990; Fullan, 1982; Guskey, 1986; Johnson & Owen, 1986; Lappan et al., 1988). Among them, Guskey's (1986) model of teachers' professional change had a substantial impact on models developed subsequently. This model emphasizes a linear sequence of change in teachers' beliefs and attitudes preceded by change in teachers' classroom practice and student learning outcomes. Reflecting and expanding the three domains of changes, Clarke and Peter (1993) proposed the Interconnected Model of Professional Growth (hereafter, the Interconnected Model), which was later further developed by Clarke and Hollingsworth (2002). Different from Guskey's model, the Interconnected Model constituted four domains, namely, the personal domain (teacher knowledge, beliefs and attitudes), the domain of practice (professional experimentation), the domain of consequence (salient outcomes), and the external domain (sources of information, stimulus or support). What made this model different from Guskey's was its emphasis on the interconnectedness (non-linear) of the four domains and the mediating agents of these changes (i.e., reflection and enactment). The model suggested change occurring in one domain led to change in another through the mediating processes of reflection and enactment. Another feature of the Interconnected Model that distinguishes it from other models was its recognition of "professional growth as an inevitable and continuing process of learning" with "multiple growth pathways between the domains" (Clarke & Hollingsworth, 2002, p. 951).

The Interconnected Model has been widely applied to studies and practices exploring teacher change (Boylan et al., 2018; Chan et al., 2019; Goldsmith et al., 2014; Justi & van Driel, 2006). It has also informed the design and development of many teacher professional development programs (Boylan et al., 2018). The study by Jin et al. (2021) was a case in point. This study investigated the effectiveness of novice-expert interaction on the professional development of TVET teachers in China. The Interconnected Model was adopted in this study to better understand what ways the external domain, in their case the support from expert teachers, impacted novice-teachers' personal domain, domain of practice, and domain of consequence. Their findings suggested that expert teachers' feedback and suggestions constituted an important external stimulus to encourage and sustain novice teachers' professional learning.

References

Arifin, Z., Nurtanto, M., Priatna, A., Kholifah, N., & Fawaid, M. (2020). Technology andragogy work content knowledge model as a new framework in vocational education: Revised technology pedagogy content knowledge model. *TEM Journal, 9*(2), 786–791. ISSN 2217-8309, https://doi.org/10.18421/TEM92-48. May 2020

Berry, B., & Cator, K. (2016). Micro-credentials driving teacher learning & leadership. Retrieved November 28, 2021.PDF

Blaschke, L. M. (2012). Heutagogy and lifelong learning: A review of heutagogical practice and self-determined learning. *The International Review of Research in Open and Distance Learning, 13*(1), 56–71. Athabasca University. https://doi.org/10.19173/irrodl.v13i1.1076

Boylan, M., Coldwell, M., Maxwell, B., & Jordan, J. (2018). Rethinking models of professional learning as tools: A conceptual analysis to inform research and practice. *Professional Development in Education, 44*(1), 120–139. https://doi.org/10.1080/19415257.2017.1306789

Brown, J. S., Collins, A., & Duguid, P. (1989). Situated cognition and the culture of learning. *Educational Researcher, 18*(1), 32–42.

Caena, F. (2011). Literature review Teachers' core competences: Requirements and development. European Commission Directorate-General for Education and Culture, pp. 28.

Cai, Q. (2021). The practical logic of the construction of the community Mechanism of university-primary and secondary school teacher training. *Contemporary Education Science, 4*, 72–81.

Calderhead, J., & Gates, P. (Eds.). (2003). *Conceptualizing reflection in teacher development* (pp. 123). Routledge.

Carr, A., Jonassen, D., Litzinger, M., & Marra, R. (1998). Good ideas to foment educational revolution: The role of systemic change in advancing situated learning. *Constructivism, and Feminist Pedagogy, Educational Technology, 38*(1–2), 5–6.

Chan, M. C. E., Anne, R., Clarke, D. J., & Clark, D. M. (2019). How do teachers learn? Different mechanisms of teacher in class learning. In G. Hine, S. Blackley, & A. Cooke (Eds.), *Mathematics education research: Impacting practice* (Proceedings of the 42nd annual conference of the Mathematics Education Research Group of Australasia) (pp. 164–171). MERGA.

Chen, J., & Zhang, J. (2009). Cognitive apprenticeship, technology, and the second educational revolution. An interview with Prof. Allan Collin, Northwestern University. *China Audio-Visual Education, 4*, 1–5.

Chen, Y. (2016). The cultivation of teachers' learning competency from the perspective of situational learning theory. *Chinese Adult Education, 24*, 9–11.

Clarke, D. J., & Peter, A. (1993). Modelling teacher change. In W. Atweh, C. Kanes, M. Carss & G. Booker (Eds.), *Contexts in mathematics education* (Proceedings of the conference of the Mathematics Education Research Group of Australasia) (pp. 167–175). MERGA.

Clarke, D., & Hollingsworth, H. (2002). Elaborating a model of teacher professional growth. *Teaching and Teacher Education, 18*, 947–967.

Cobb, P., Wood, T., & Yackel, E. (1990). Classrooms as learning environments for teachers and researchers. In R. B. Davis, C. A. Mayer, & N. Noddings (Eds.), *Constructivist views on the teaching and learning of mathematics* (pp. 125–146). National Council of Teachers of Mathematics.

Collins, A., Brown, J. S., & Holum, A. (1991). Cognitive apprenticeship: Making thinking visible. *American Educator, 15*(3), 6–11.

Collins, A., Brown, J. S., & Newman, S. E. (1989). Cognitive apprenticeship: Teaching the craft of reading, writing and mathematics! In L. B. Resnick (Ed.), *Knowing, learning, and instruction: Essa in honor of Robert Glaser*. Erlbaum.

Commission of the European Communities. (2006). *Adult learning: It is never too late to learn.* COM (2006). 614 final. Brussels, October 23, 2006.

Cox, S., & Graham, C. R. (2009). Diagramming TPACK in practice: Using an elaborated model of the TPACK framework to analyze and depict teacher knowledge. *TechTrends, 53*(5), 60–69.

Crow, T. (2017). *Micro-credentials for impact: Holding professional learning to high standards*. https://learningforward.org/wp-content/uploads/2017/08/micro-credentials-for-impact.pdf

Dubé, L., Bourhis, A., & Jacob, R. (2005). The impact of structuring characteristics on the launching of virtual communities of practice. *Journal of Organizational Change Management, 18*(2), 145–166. https://doi.org/10.1108/09534810510589570

European Commission (2020). A European approach to micro-credentials—Output of the microcredentials higher education consultation group—Final report. European Commission, Brussels.

Fadel, C., Bialik, M., & Trilling, B. (2015). *Four-dimensional education. The competencies learners need to succeed*. Center for Curriculum Redesign.

Feiman-Nemser, S. (2001). From preparation to practice: Designing a continuum to strengthen and sustain teaching. *Teachers College Record, 103*(6), 1013–1055.

Fullan, M. (1982). *The meaning of educational change*. Teachers College Press.

Goldsmith, L. T., Doerr, H. M., & Lewis, C. C. (2014). Mathematics teachers' learning: A conceptual framework and synthesis of research. *Journal of Mathematics Teacher Education, 17*(1), 5–17. https://doi.org/10.1007/s10857-013-9245-4

Grant, C. A. (2008). Teacher capacity. In Cochran-Smith, M., Feiman-Nemser, S., & McIntyre, D. (Eds.), *Handbook of research on teacher education. Enduring questions in changing contexts* (pp. 113–127). Routledge/Taylor & Francis.

Gu, X., Du, H., Peng, H., & Zhu, Z. (2021). The theoretical framework, practical path, development vein and future prospect of wisdom education. *Journal of East China Normal University (education Science), 8*, 20–32.

Guskey, T. R. (1986). Staff development and the process of teacher change. *Educational Researcher, 15*(5), 5–12.

Guthrie, H. (2010). Professional development in the vocational education and training workforce. Occasional paper. National Centre for Vocational Education Research Ltd. PO Box 8288, Stational Arcade, Adelaide, SA 5000, Australia.

Han, X., Ge, L., & Cheng, J. (2019). Introduction to the research of vocational education informatization (pp. 195). Tsinghua University.

Hoel, T., & Mason, J. (2018). Stands for smart education-towards a development framework. *Smart Learning Environments, 5*, 3. https://doi.org/10.1186/s40561-018-0052-3

https://www.oecd-ilibrary.org/education/pisa_19963777

Hu, F. (2019). Towards real situation: Exploration of new teacher training under the guidance of cognitive apprenticeship. *Management of Primary and Secondary Schools, 4*, 43–45.

Illeris, K. (2011). Workplaces and learning. In M. Malloch, L. Cairns, K. Evans, & B. N. O'Connor (Eds.), *The Sage handbook of workplace learning* (pp. 32–45). Sage.

Jameson, J., Ferrell, G., Kelly, J., Walker, S., & Ryan, M. (2006). Building trust and shared knowledge in communities of e-learning practice: Collaborative leadership in the JISC eLISA and CAMEL lifelong learning projects. *British Journal of Educational Technology, 37*(6), 949–967.

Jin, X., Li, T., Meirink, J., van der Want, A., & Admiraal, W. (2021). Learning from novice–expert interaction in teachers' continuing professional development. *Professional Development in Education, 47*(5), 745–762. https://doi.org/10.1080/19415257.2019.1651752

Johnson, N., & Owen, J. (1986). *The two cultures revisited: Interpreting messages from models of teaching and clinical supervision to encourage improvement in teaching*. Paper presented to the Australian Educational Research Association Annual Conference, Melbourne.

Justi, R., & van Driel, J. (2006). The use of the Interconnected model of teacher professional growth for understanding the development of science teachers' knowledge on models and modelling. *Teaching and Teacher Education, 22*(4), 437–450. https://doi.org/10.1016/j.tate.2005.11.011

Kato, S., Galán-Muros, V., & Weko, T. (2020). The emergence of alternative credentials. *OECD Education Working Papers, No. 216*. OECD Publishing, Paris. https://doi.org/10.1787/b741f39e-en

Kietzmann, J., Plangger, K., Eaton, B., Heilgenberg, K., Pitt, L., & Berthon, P. (2013). Mobility at work: A typology of mobile communities of practice and contextual ambidexterity (PDF).

Journal of Strategic Information Systems, 3(4), 282–297. https://doi.org/10.1016/j.jsis.2013.03.003.S2CID3714450

Knowles, M. (1978). Andragogy: Adult learning theory in perspective. *Community College Review, 5*(9), 9–20.

Koehler, M. J., & Mishra, P. (2005). What happens when teachers design educational technology? The development of technological pedagogical content knowledge. *Journal of Educational Computing Research, 32*(2), 131–152. https://doi.org/10.2190/0EW7-01WB-BKHL-QDYV

Koehler, M. J., & Mishra, P. (2009). What is technological pedagogical content knowledge? *Contemporary Issues in Technology and Teacher Education (CITE Journal), 9*(1), 60–70.

Kong, S. (2018). Community of practice: An effective way to ESL teacher professional development in vocational colleges. *English Language Teaching, 11*(7).

Koper, R. (2014). Conditions for effective smart learning environments. *Smart Learning Environments, 1*, 5. https://doi.org/10.1186/s40561-014-0005-4

Koster, B., & Dengerink, J. J. (2008). Professional standards for teacher educators: how to deal with complexity, ownership and function. Experiences from the Netherlands. *European Journal of Teacher Education, 31*(2), 135–149.

Lahn, L. C., & Nore, H. (2019). Large-scale studies of holistic professional competence in vocational education and training (VET). The case of Norway. *International Journal for Research in Vocational Education and Training, 6*(2), 132–152.

Lappan, G., Fitzgerald, W., Phillips, E., Winter, M. J., Lanier, P., Madsen-Nason, A., Even, R., Lee, B., Smith, J., & Weinberg, D. (1988). The middle grades mathematics project. The challenge: Good mathematics—taught well (Final report of the National Science Foundation for Grant #MDR8318218). East Lansing, MI: Michigan State University.

Lave, J., & Wenger, E. (1991). In Wang, W. (Ed.), *Situated learning—Legitimate peripheral participation* (Trans. 2004). East China Normal University Press.

Lindeman, E. (1926). *The meaning of adult education*. New Republic Inc.

Lu, W. (2010). The enlightenment of adult learning theory on teacher training. *Continuing Education Research, 1*, 104–105.

Merriam, S., & Bierema, L. (2014). *Adult learning: Linking theory to practice*. Jossey Bass.

Merriam, S. B. (2008). Adult learning theory for the twenty-first century. *New Directions for Adult and Continuing Education, 119*. Fall 2008 Wiley Periodicals, Inc. Published online in Wiley InterScience (www.interscience.wiley.com). https://doi.org/10.1002/ace.309

Mezirow, J. (2000). *Learning as transformation. Critical perspectives on a theory in progress*. Jossey-Bass.

Miao, Q., Ma, Y., Wenxiang, F., & Qiaomei, D. (2016). A survey on TPACK competency of vocational college teachers and cultivation strategies—Taking Chongqing as an example. *Vocational and Technical Education, 37*(36), 51–57.

OECD. (2001). http://200.6.99.248/~bru487cl/files/libros/Tendencias/pdf/960103 1e.pdf

OECD. (2021). Micro-credential innovations in higher education: Who, what and why? *OECD Education Policy Perspectives, 39*. OECD Publishing, Paris. https://doi.org/10.1787/f14ef041-en

Ouyang, H. (2003). The concept and connotation of vocational education. *Education and Vocation, 1*, 24–26.

Pedersen, K. W. (2017). Supporting collaborative and continuing professional development in education for sustainability through a communities of practice approach. *International Journal of Sustainability in Higher Education, 18*(5), 681–696. © Emerald Publishing Limited, 1467-6370. https://doi.org/10.1108/IJSHE-02-2016-0033

Pei, M., & Li, X. (2014). The interpretation of "teacher learning" from the perspective of adult learning theory: Returning to teacher's adult identity. *Teacher Education Research, 26*(6), 16–21.

Peng, M. (2014). The effective training of "double-qualified" teachers in higher vocational colleges–based on the perspective of adult learning theory. *Vocational and Technical Education, 35*(31), 66–69.

Pór, G. (2004). *Liberating the innovation value of communities of practice. Report written in collaboration with Erik van Bekkum*. Community Intelligence Ltd.

Qin, X., & Zeng, W. (2019). Training of young teachers' teaching ability in applied colleges from the perspective of cognitive apprenticeship. *Education & Occupation, 14*, 84–87.

Ran, X., & Cai, R. (2017). Research on TPACK Knowledge Structure of "Dual-qualification" Teachers in Secondary Vocational Schools—Based on Survey for 5 Secondary Vocational Schools in Fujian Province (in Chinese). *Vocational and Technical Education, 38*(34), 38–44.

Rauner, F., Heinemann, L., & Hauschildt, U. (2013a). Measuring occupational competences: Concept, method and findings of the COMET project. In L. Deitmer, U. Hauschildt, F. Rauner, & H. Zelloth (Eds.), *The architecture of innovative apprenticeship* (159–175). Springer Science CBusiness Media.

Rauner, F., Heinemann, L., Maurer, A., Haasler, B., Erdwien, B., & Martens, T. (2013b). *Competence-development and assessment in TVET: Theoretical framework and empirical results (COMET)*. Springer Verlag.

Rauner, F. (2021). *Measuring and developing professional competences in COMET: Method manual*. Springer Singapore.

Rychen, D. S., & Salganik, L. H. (2003). *Key Competencies for a successful life and a well-functioning society*. Hogrefe & Huber.

See: https://en.unesco.org/sites/default/files/tvet.pdf

Seet, P. S., & Jones, J. T. (2021). Extending micro-credentials to micro-apprenticeships for the fourth industrial revolution: Enhancing vocational education and training in the post-pandemic's 'new normal'. *Journal of Teaching and Learning for Graduate Employability, 12*(1), 39–43. https://doi.org/10.21153/jtlge2021vol12no1art1317

Spector, J. M. (2014). Conceptualizing the emerging field of smart learning environments. *Smart Learning Environments, 1*(1), 5–10. https://doi.org/10.1186/s40561-014-0002-7

Sterrett, S. E., Hawkins, S. R., & Hertweck, M. L., & Schreiber, J. (2015). Developing communities of interprofessional practice using a communities of practice framework for interprofessional education. *Nurse Educator, 40*(1), E1–E4

Tang, D., & Bai, L. (2021). Re-understanding and re-education of TPACK for vocational educational teachers in 5 G era. *Research on Vocational Education, 8*, 83–89.

Tang, S. (2006). Theoretical framework for solving the problems of rural teacher development in China. *Journal of Henan Normal University (philosophy and Social Science Edition), 3*, 188–191.

UNESCO (1996). Learning: The treasure within. Report of the International Commission on Education for the 21st Century. UNESCO, Paris.

Wei, F., & Zhu, Z. (2017). Micro-credentials: A new way for competency-based teacher development. *Open Education Research, 3*, 71–79.

Wenger, E., McDermott, R., & Snyder, W. (2002). *Cultivating communities of practice*. Harvard Business School Press.

Williamson McDiarmid, G., & Clevenger-Bright, M. (2008). Rethinking teacher capacity. In M. Cochran Smith, S. Feiman-Nemser, & D. Mc Intyre, (Eds.), *Handbook of research on teacher education. Enduring questions in changing contexts*. Abingdon, Taylor & Francis.

Xie, L., & Li, N. (2006). The enlightenment of situational learning theory to teacher training. *Teacher Training in Primary and Secondary Schools, 11*, 16–18.

Yang, X., & Chang, B. (2010). An epistemological analysis of educational practice: Based on constructivist theory. *Foreign Educational Research, 11*, 46–51.

Yu, Q. (2015). Improvement of teacher qualification for secondary vocational education teachers of general courses. *Teacher Education Research, 27*(3), 25–30.

Zhang, L. (2001). Teachers' reflection and strategies. *Educational Research, 12*, 17–21.

Zhang, Q., & Rong, G. (2011). Informatization drives the modernization of vocational education. *Vocational and Technical Education, 36*, 74–77.

Zhang, Q., & Yang, S. (2005). Cognitive apprenticeship in the context of situational learning. *Modern Distance Education Research, 4*, 42–45 + 72.

Zhao, Y., & Ko, J. (2018). Workplace learning in the professional development of vocational education teachers. *Studia Paedagogica, 23*(2). www.studiapaedagogica.cz. https://doi.org/10.5817/SP2018-2-4. Accessed January 10, 2023.

Zhao, Z., & Rauner, F. (2020). COMET professional competency measurement method manual. *Journal of Education, 16*(1), 62.

Zhao, Z., & Zhuang, R. (2012). Research and development of the curriculum for the secondary teachers' qualification. *Education and Training, 5*, 12–15.

Zhong, Z. (2008). *The teaching mode innovation in colleges—From perspective of teaching design* (p. 146). Education Science Press.

Zhong, Z. (2015). *Self-management of distance learners* (p. 16). Central Radio and Television University Press.

Zhong, Z. (2020a). *Be a wise teacher of technology empowerment*. Jiangxi Normal University.

Zhong, Z. (2020b). New situation of teacher education development under artificial intelligence background. *Chinese Teachers, 11*, 33–37.

Zhong, Z., & Zhu, R. (2011). Community of practice: Concept, characteristics, construction principles and learning process design. *Read and Write, 7*, 1–3.

Zhou, J. (2017). The reform of teacher training mode from the perspective of situational learning theory. *Education Theory and Practice, 37*(4), 33–37.

Zhu, S. (2004). Foreign teacher education and enlightenment. *Continuing Education, 9*, 61–62.

Zhu, Z. T., & Bin, H. (2012). Smart education: A new paradigm in educational technology. *Telecommunication Education, 12*, 3–15.

Zhu, Z. T., Yu, M. H., & Riezebos, P. (2016). A research framework of smart education. *Smart Learning Environments*, 1–17. https://doi.org/10.1186/s40561-016-0026-2

Zhu, Z., & Peng, H. (2021). Innovation and development of technology-empowered wisdom education—Interview with Professor Zhu Zhiting, pioneer of wisdom education in China. *Journal of Teacher Education, 4*, 21–29.

Zhu, Z., & Wei, F. (2018). Education informatization 2.0: Smart education starts, smart education leads. *Audio-Visual Education Research, 9*, 5–16.

Open Access This chapter is licensed under the terms of the Creative Commons Attribution-NonCommercial-NoDerivatives 4.0 International License (http://creativecommons.org/licenses/by-nc-nd/4.0/), which permits any noncommercial use, sharing, distribution and reproduction in any medium or format, as long as you give appropriate credit to the original author(s) and the source, provide a link to the Creative Commons license and indicate if you modified the licensed material. You do not have permission under this license to share adapted material derived from this chapter or parts of it.

The images or other third party material in this chapter are included in the chapter's Creative Commons license, unless indicated otherwise in a credit line to the material. If material is not included in the chapter's Creative Commons license and your intended use is not permitted by statutory regulation or exceeds the permitted use, you will need to obtain permission directly from the copyright holder.

Chapter 3
Professional Competencies in TVET: Framework, Indicators and Assessment Instrument

Junfeng Diao, Xibin Han, Qian Zhou, and Yuping Wang

3.1 Introduction

This chapter starts with a discussion of the challenges in and need for developing TVET teachers' digital teaching competencies. Informed by existing research and practices in developing professional competencies for teachers, in particular for TVET teachers, we then propose a framework that identifies core competencies required of in-service TVET teachers and practitioners in the digital age in Sect. 3.2. In Sect. 3.3, this framework is further expanded by the proposal of indicators for each of the proposed core competencies, which form the basis for an instrument developed for assessing these competencies. Section 3.4 suggests ways of how the framework, indicators, and assessment instrument can be used to guide and support TVET teachers' professional development.

3.1.1 Challenges Facing the Development of Digital Teaching Competencies for TVET Teachers

In the last 20 years, two kinds of transformation through technology have fundamentally changed the landscape of TVET: the transformation of TVET through ICT

J. Diao (✉)
School of Education, Hainan Normal University, Haikou, China
e-mail: 920268@hainnu.edu.cn

X. Han · Q. Zhou
Institute of Education, Tsinghua University, Beijing, China

Y. Wang
School of Humanities, Languages and Social Science, Griffith University, Brisbane, Australia

and the technological transformation of the world of work. Transforming TVET through ICT has been accelerated since the Third International Congress on Technical and Vocational Education and Training held in Shanghai in 2012 (UNESCO, 2012a, 2012b). As a result, digitalization, blended, and online learning have become the catchphrases in TVET, although the degree of their implementation differs from country to country (Subrahmanyam, 2022). Such a transformation brings with it a need for teachers in TVET to constantly update and expand their knowledge and skills, in particular, technological competence needed to facilitate and innovate teaching and learning. At the same time, the technological transformation happening in industry calls for a constant curriculum upgrade, and/or even a curriculum overhaul in some cases to foster new skills and/or professions needed by today's industry such as greening skills for sustainable developments. Are TVET teachers technologically, pedagogically, and even psychologically prepared to meet these challenges? Are there effective ongoing and sustainable professional development programs available to help TVET teachers to identify and develop the competencies needed in today's vocational education? The most recent UNESCO trends mapping study titled Digital Skills Development in TVET Teacher Training reveals that there were tremendous issues facing TVET teachers and trainers both before and during Covid-19. Among them was the lack of training in digital skills as a key challenge. This challenge was strongly linked to the lack of digital access and infrastructure, and to the lack of trained trainers with the required skills and knowledge for facilitating the digital competence development of TVET teachers and trainers. The study further reported that existing digital skills training programs tended to (a) focus on the use of tools for teaching TVET rather than on alternative forms of course delivery, (b) teach teachers/ trainers how to use technology rather than how to apply different digital options, (c) not be targeted to reach a multigenerational teacher/ trainer workforce, and/or (d) lack relevant content" (Subrahmanyam, 2022, p. 15).

In terms of levels of digital teaching competencies measured by the four-stage ICT adoption model (i.e., emerging, adopting, infusing and transforming) proposed by UNEVOC (UNESCO-UNEVOC,), teachers and trainers today in most cases were found at the levels of "applying" and "infusing." (p. 19) This was because existing professional development programs seldom provided them "with the level and depth of digital and pedagogical skills" demanded by teaching transformation (Subrahmanyam, 2022, p. 19). It was further revealed in this study that there still existed a fear of and resistance to changes and to the adoption of new technologies in teaching among TVET teachers as far as attitude was concerned.

In addition to acquiring digital teaching competence, TVET teacher are also facing the challenges of upgrading their existing knowledge, skills, and pedagogy and develop new subject matter and/or disciplinary expertise. This challenge has largely brought about by the fast-changing industry and the goals for sustainable development and green economies. Today, many traditional occupations are becoming obsolete and new industries are replacing the old. As the main producers of future labour force, vocational education is responsible for aligning education and training with the sustainable development goals and developing future workforce who is capable of responding effectively to the principles and needs of sustainable development agenda. Therefore, incumbent upon TVET teachers is to develop knowledge, skills, and competencies needed for green occupations, economies, and societies.

Clearly, to help TVET teachers to meet these challenges, systematic and continuing professional development is urgently needed. Against this background, we propose a new competency framework, relevant competency indicators, and an assessment instrument to help today's TVET teachers upgrade and develop the competencies needed in the digital age.

3.1.2 The Need for a New Framework of Digital Teaching Competencies for TVET Teachers

Since the turn of the century, especially since Covid-19, supporting TVET teachers in developing digital competencies has become the centre of attention as far as vocational institutional policies and efforts are concerned. On the part of individual teachers, despite all the challenges mentioned above, an ongoing effort has been to constantly increase their agency so that they can take better advantage of the opportunities that educational technology can offer for pedagogical innovation. There have been a number of guidelines, standards, and competency frameworks guiding the institutional and individual teachers' efforts in teachers' professional development (see Becker, 2010; Berliner, 2004; Diao & Yang, 2021; Diep & Hartmann, 2016; Latchem, 2017; Rauner et al., 2013b; Rauner, 2021; Subrahmanyam, 2022; Wagiran et al., 2019a, 2019b). Among them, the COMET framework proposed by Rauner et al. (2013b) and the test instruments subsequently developed based on this framework have been widely evaluated and adopted in TVET teacher professional development. A more detailed discussion on this framework is contained in Sect. 2.2.2. A more recent study specifically addressing TVET teachers' competency development in the Industry 4.0 era is found in Jafar et al. (2020). Based on a comprehensive literature review and the analysis of TVET teachers' competencies explored in nine most relevant studies, Jafar et al. proposed a TVET Teacher Professional Competencies framework in the Industry 4.0 era. The framework is composed of 5 dimensions: technical, non-technical, personal attributes, motive, and mental and physical. Comprehensive as it is, the model is static and merely presents a list of competencies required of TVET teachers today. Without criteria indicative of the competency levels that a teacher can/should achieve and without projecting a dynamic competency progression phase by phase, the framework does not present itself as a user-friendly tool to assess TVET teachers' competency development. Similar deficiencies also applied to most existing competency frameworks for TVET teachers. Here we concur with Diep and Hartmann (2016) that "competence of vocational teacher is still a complex, ill-structured domain facing the fast-change world with the tendency of sustainable development" (p. 7). We believe high time that a more operational, adaptable, and easy-to-use framework with clear competency indicators is developed. Informed by existing literature and new insights from the most recent practices in the digital age, we propose here a TVET teacher competency framework and developed relevant competency indicators and a competency assessment instrument with the aim to:

- reflect the key competencies required of TVET teachers in the digital age.
- provide a reference point for developing ongoing professional development programs.
- provide an easy-to-use and adaptable instrument for TVET teachers to self-assess their competency levels.
- help individual teachers to formulate short-term and long-term career objectives and plans.
- help individual teachers to develop self-development strategies.
- contribute to institutional policy making in regard to teachers' professional development initiative, strategies and support structures and mechanisms.
- contribute to national policy formulation relating to vocational education reform, digital transformation and professional development for TVET teachers and trainers.
- provide a basis for future research to update the competencies contained in the proposed framework and integrate new competencies and criteria to meet the for-ever changing needs of industry.

3.2 Rationales for Proposing a Competency Framework for TVET Teachers in the Digital Age

This section consists of two parts. Section 3.2.1 reviews the relevant literature on the roles that TVET teachers play in the digital age, with the aim of exploring the competencies required of TVET teachers today. Section 3.2.2 reviews existing approaches to the examination of teacher professional development trajectory in terms of stages of development. Discussions in these two sections lead to our proposal of a digital teaching competency framework for today's TVET teachers in Sect. 3.3. Discussions contained in Sect. 3.2 also informs our proposal of TVET teachers' competency indicators and a competency assessment instrument in Sect. 3.4.

3.2.1 Exploring TVET Teachers' Competencies in the Digital Age: A Multi-role Perspective

In the digital age, TVET teachers are required to play multiple roles to meet the demands of the age. In this section, we focus on four of these roles to explore professional competencies that TVET teachers need to develop today. These competencies are discussed in the context of TVET teachers as teachers by profession, vocational practitioners and trainers, digital citizens and lifelong learners. The review on the basic tenants in teacher competencies contained in Sect. 2.1.2 supplements the discussion here.

TVET Teachers' Competencies as a Teacher by Profession

TVET teachers, first and foremost, is an educator with the same basic competency requirements as those in schools and higher education. Different lenses and approaches have been adopted to exposit competencies for teachers in general. For example, from the iceberg model perspective, competencies for teachers can include knowledge, skills, social role, self-image, traits, and motives (London leadership academy., n.d.). On the other hand, the psychological perspective of teachers' competencies emphasizes teachers' value systems, psychological wellbeing, personality, and ethics. Research on pedagogy often concerns teachers' competencies in curriculum development and delivery. Models and approaches have been developed to guide the developmental process of curriculum development. Among them, the ADDIE model is perhaps the most commonly used (Morrison, 2010). ADDIE is the acronym for Analysis, Design, Develop, Implementation, and Evaluation. As far as TVET teachers' competencies are concerned, curriculum development has its own unique concerns and requirements, in comparison to that in general education. Quality curriculum design in the digital age requires a good understanding of the potential of ICT in meeting learners' needs, in addition to a sufficient command of vocational theories, knowledge, and relevant vocational skills. Curriculum design should also be informed by an analysis of learner and industry needs. Diao and Yang (2021) believed that curriculum development for TVET teachers should be the concerted efforts of the TVET teachers and experts from relevant industries, and it should be supported by institutional professional development communities. They suggested four key components in TVET curriculum development: analysis of industry needs and requirements, analysis of specific task needs, course development, and project development. Among them, needs analysis informs course and project design. Integrating the needs of industry into curriculum design has never been more crucial than it is today. The twenty-first century industry is experiencing tremendous changes almost every day, especially in the process of achieving the goals of sustainable developments.

Curriculum delivery in TVET also has its own unique demands, strategies, and approaches. While different pedagogical approaches are adopted in different subject areas and countries, the learner-centered approach is gaining prominence in TVET. This approach sees teachers as learning facilitators rather than instructors, and students as active agents in learning rather than passive receivers of instructions (Hannafin et al., 2014). Guided by this approach, we argue here that TVET teachers today are required to develop facilitating skills to support student contextual, authentic, and hands-on learning through the use of ICT. This is a process of developing students' capacity in problem solving, critical thinking, and autonomous learning. In a typical TVET classroom, students' engagement in specific, real-life task completion through hands-on learning is often a regular part of the classroom activities. Blended learning also requires TVET teachers to facilitate learning and training in a multimodal environment and use technology in a pedagogically sound manner. Teaching in TVET today also includes collaborating and negotiating with industry for opportunities of vocational skill training and upskilling.

TVET Teachers' Competencies as a Vocational Practitioner and Skill Trainer

The strong link between the TVET system and industry places special demands on TVET teachers and their professional development. It also creates confusion about the roles of TVET teachers. Existing research on TVET teachers' competencies features an ongoing dialogue on the dual nature of this profession encompassing their pedagogical expertise as a teacher and vocational knowledge and skills as a trainer/tradesperson (Tyler & Dymock, 2021). To put it simply, TVET teachers need to play the dual role of teaching domain knowledge and theories and training students on vocational skills. Terms such as "double reference" (Becker & Spottl, 2019, p. 7) and "dual professionalism" (Avis & Orr, 2014, p. 1101) are often used to describe such a dual nature of this profession. This dualism has set the TVET teachers apart from teachers in general education and has received increasing attention from TVET professionals in recent years. This is because the ever-changing needs in today's workplace require TVET teachers to update their knowledge and skills in order to stay abreast with what is needed in today's labor market. Köpsén (2014) argued for "a contemporary and modern vocational identity that addresses the current demands for vocational knowledge and skills as well as values and attitudes" (p. 209). The competencies required of TVET teachers as a practitioner and trainer include both pedagogic capability of imparting theories and knowledge to students in a specific subject area, and occupational capacity of applying practical knowledge (e.g., procedural knowledge) to training students on vocational skills and workplace ethics. To Diao and Yang (2021), domain theories and knowledge were critically important as they reflected teachers' mastery of the subject area contents, and their understanding of industry and reflection of workplace practices. Vocational capacity is thus a core competency for TVET teachers. It includes the capacity to communicate with industry, practical occupational expertise, and the ability to serve the needs of industry.

TVET Teachers' Competencies as a Digital Citizen

In the digital age, teachers are digital citizens. However, digital competence for teachers, including TVET teachers, encapsulates much more than what is prescribed for an average digital citizen. In addition to possessing the basic digital literacy to survive in society as everyone else does, TVET teachers need to acquire knowledge and capacities to enhance and support student learning with technology. As exposited in the widely used TPCK framework (see discussion in Sect. 2.2.1), teachers today first need to possess basic knowledge of and ability to use a variety of essential ICTs to support/enable student learning. More importantly, they need to acquire Technological Content Knowledge (TCK) to be able to identify appropriate technologies for specific content design and development for realizing specific learning goals. Finally, teachers need to develop Technological Pedagogical Knowledge (TPK) to be able to apply appropriate technologies to enhance and innovate pedagogy and student learning. In other words, technology should be applied in a pedagogically effective manner to make learning more flexible, interactive, and inclusive. Similar emphases have been repeatedly conveyed in recent studies on TVET teachers' competency development (Hodges et al., 2020; Subrahmanyam, 2022). According to *Digital Campus Specifications for Vocational Institutions* published by the Ministry of Education, China, digital competency for teachers consists of four dimensions: the awareness of technological advancements and attitudes towards ICT adoption, technological knowledge and skills, application of ICT to teaching and teaching innovation, and social responsibilities (Ministry of Education of the PRC, 2020). All of the above discussed technological competencies are particularly relevant to TVET teachers, with a strong emphasis on the fluent use of their digital competencies to facilitate authentic experiential and contextual learning and training in real world settings (Liu, & Yin, 2014).

TVET Teachers' Competencies as a Life-Long Learner

Lifelong learning has never been so integral to our lives in the twenty-first century as we need to constantly update our knowledge and skills to adapt to the rapidly changing vocational education, society and world of work. Lifelong learning should be an indispensable part of TVET teachers' professional life.

First, they need to respond to the transformation taking place in industry such as the new skill requirements for a green economy (Diep & Hartmann, 2016). To TVET, such a transformation means many previously highly demanded disciplinary areas and courses such as traditional manufacturing and processing, are being replaced by new subject areas and courses such as artificial intelligence and green technologies. These changes require TVET teachers to constantly update their existing curricula and develop new curricula to stay current with industry developments and meet the needs of current and future students.

Second, the digital transformation taking place in TVET also impels teachers to constantly advance their technological knowledge and digital teaching skills to respond to new demands in facilitating student learning and training. Thus, lifelong learning is part and parcel of TVET teachers' professional life. There is a dual focus in TVET teachers' lifelong learning: self-development to become a lifelong learner themselves and helping students to become lifelong learners. As a lifelong learner, TVET teachers need keep themselves up to date on new pedagogical theories, technological development, in particular, the development of environmentally friendly technologies, as argued by Diep and Hartmann (2016). In addition, they also need to develop competencies to help students to learn how to learn so that students can

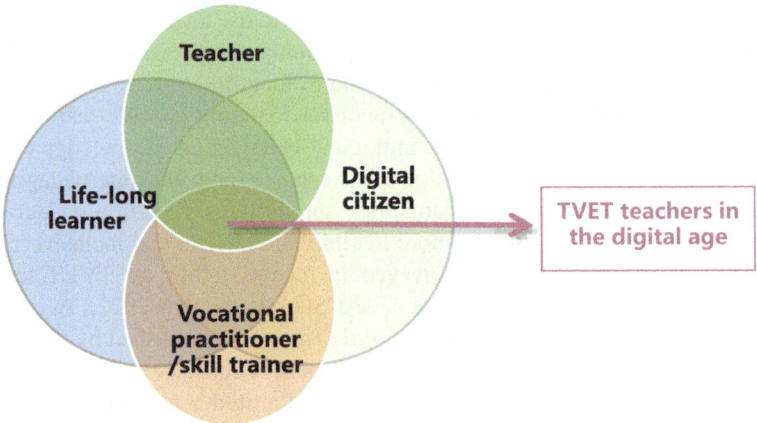

Fig. 3.1 The multi-role identity of TVET teachers in the digital age

develop lifelong learning strategies from an early age. Such strategies help students to become flexible, adaptable, and open-minded future workforce. While technological advancements have made lifelong learning a necessity, it also has great potential to assist and enable lifelong learning, making it ubiquitous, as the distinction between formal, informal, in-class and out-of-class learning is fast becoming blurry.

To summarize, TVET teachers in the digital age are teachers by profession, vocational practitioners and skill trainers, digital citizens and lifelong learners. This multi-role identity is depicted in Fig. 3.1.

On the basis of the above discussion, this handbook proposes a framework of teaching competencies for TVET teachers in the digital age. It consists of six constructs: curriculum improvement/development, facilitating learning, vocational knowledge and expertise, vocational capacity, digital competence and competence for research, and self-development. Among them, curriculum improvement/development and facilitating learning are the basic competencies that should be possessed by a teacher; vocational knowledge, expertise, and vocational capacity are the competencies required of a vocational practitioner and skill trainer. As a digital citizen, TVET teachers should possess not only basic digital literacy, but also digital proficiency to engage and support student learning and training. As a life-long learner, the capacity to research and self-develop is crucial.

3.2.2 The Stages of TVET Teachers' Competency Development

As far as Teacher Career Cycle theory is concerned, the models proposed by Fessler (1991) and Huberman (1992) are often cited to guide research on teachers' professional life development trajectory. Fessler's model consists of eight stages: preservice, induction, competency building, enthusiastic and growing, career frustration, career winddown, and career exit. The preservice stage in a teacher's career cycle was excluded from Huberman's seven stage model that began from career entry, moving up to survival and discovery, stabilization, experimentation and diversification, stock-taking and interrogations, serenity and conservatism, and disengagement (serene or bitter).

Fuller's Concerns-based model,, (see Fuller, 1969; Fuller & Bown, 1975; for a review see Rutherford & Hall, 1990) is a three-stage approach to teacher professional growth sequenced as concerns about self in stage one, concerns about tasks/ situations in stage two, and concerns about students in stage three. This model has been "dedicated to understanding the developmental dynamics of pre-service and early in-service teachers" (Conway & Clark, 2003, p. 466). In the late 1970s and early 1980s, the Concerns Based Adoption Model (CBAM) was proposed by Hall and others (see Hall & Hord, 1987, 2006; Hall & Loucks, 1978; Loucks et al., 1975) in the context of educational change and innovation adoption. Building on the premise that change is a process, not an event, this model "recognizes educational change is multifaceted and involves the complex and dynamic interplay between people, organizations, systems and processes" (Saunders, 2012, p. 187). There are three dimensions in this model: stages of concern, levels of use, and innovation configurations. Although this model has been widely adopted in the design and implementation of professional development programs in many educational settings, to date, not much has been reported regarding its application to TVET teachers' professional development, with the exception of the study by Saunders (2012).

From a cognitive development perspective, a progression approach has been widely adopted to project a teacher's competence trajectory from novice to expert. Dreyfus and Dreyfus (1986) proposed a five-stage theory of teacher development from (1) novice, (2) advanced beginner, (3) competent, (4) proficient to (5) expert stages. Berliner (2004) commented that the first three stages were a "progression with identifiable behaviours and modes of thinking that are acquired by teachers over an extended period of time," while the boundary between the last two stages are often overlap and hard to distinguish (p. 22). Berliner's research adopted this model to investigate and confirm traits of expert teachers.

This model was also adopted by Rauner (2007) to illustrate the competence development stages for TVET teachers. He also discussed four developmental learning areas corresponding to a teacher's development from novice to expert. Four types of practical knowledge are covered in these four learning areas and they are sequenced as "orientation and overview of knowledge" for novice progressing to advanced beginner, "coherent knowledge" for advanced beginner advancing to competent teacher, "detailed and functional knowledge" for competent moving to proficient teacher, and "experience-based specialized knowledge" for proficient teacher becoming expert. These stages, learning areas, and scopes of knowledge help us to identify the "thresholds and stages in the development of occupational competence and identity; they also have a didactic function in the development of work-related and structurally oriented vocational courses" (Rauner, 2007, p. 55).

Drawing on research and evidence of good practice and in consultation with academic staff and experts and wider academic community, the Royal Academy of Engineering in the UK (2018) published its Career Framework for University Teaching. This framework entails four progressive levels in regard to teaching and leadership in teaching and learning. Level 1 involves 'the effective teacher' and delineates the threshold level of teaching competence with key adjectives such as "conscientious," "reflective," and "effective." Level 2 is "the skilled and collegial teacher" that emphasizes "an evidence-informed approach" to their professional development and the provision of mentorship to their colleagues (p. 38). There are two pathways at Level 3, "the institutional leader" and "the scholarly teacher," with the former contributing to "enhancing the environment for inclusion and excellence in teaching and learning within and beyond their institution" and the latter contributing to "pedagogical knowledge by engaging with and contributing to scholarly research which, in turn, influence educational practice within and beyond their institution" (p. 38). Level 4 includes the national and global leader in teaching that places a strong emphasis on national and global leadership in teaching and pedagogical research.

In different ways and to varying degrees, these three types of models inform our classification of the developmental stages contained in the TVET teachers' competency framework proposed in this handbook. In particular, our four-stage classification (i.e., beginner, competent, proficient, and expert stages) draws on the Concerns Based Adoption model and cognitive development frameworks. This will be discussed in more detail in the section below.

3.3 Proposing a Competency Framework for TVET Teachers in the Digital Age

The above discussions on TVET teachers' roles and the stages of professional development led to our proposal of a framework for TVET teachers' competencies in the digital age. It consists of six constructs and four developmental stages (see Table 3.1).

Table 3.1 A framework of TVET teachers' competency in the digital age

	Beginner	Competent teacher	Proficient teacher	Expert
Curriculum improvement/ development	Improve/develop blended learning curricula with support	Improve/develop blended learning curricula with less or without support	Innovate blended learning curricula informed by new theories, practices, and industry needs	Innovate and transform curricula informed by new theories, practices, and industry needs
Facilitating learning and training	Facilitate learning and training in blended mode with support	Facilitate learning and training in blended mode with less or without support	Innovate blended learning and training pedagogy based on learners' needs	Innovate and transform blended learning and training pedagogy with new knowledge, theories, and skills
Vocational knowledge and expertise	Apply vocational knowledge and expertise in blended learning and training with support	Update and apply vocational knowledge and expertise to solve problems in blended learning and training with less or without support	Update and apply vocational knowledge and expertise in an integrated manner in blended learning and training	Integrate vocational knowledge and expertise to innovate and transform blended teaching, learning, and skill training
Vocational capacity	Gain new understanding of occupational skills needed by industry	Apply new understanding and knowledge of occupational skills to blended learning and training	Update and apply occupational knowledge and skills to training in an integrated manner	Transform and innovate occupational skills learning and training in collaboration with industry
Digital competence	Use basic ICT in blended learning and skill training with support	Apply ICT pedagogically to improve blended learning and skill training	Infuse ICT with pedagogical approaches innovatively to improve blended learning and skill training	Transform teaching, learning, and training with ICT and lead TVET to new practices
Research and self development	Conduct teaching-related research and self-development with support	Conduct teaching-related research and self-development with less or without support	Conduct research on teaching innovation and design self-development plans and strategies	Develop forward thinking and conduct peer mentoring on research and teaching innovation

3.3.1 Rationale for Each of the Six Constructs of the Proposed Framework

As shown in Table 3.1, there are six key constructs for TVET teachers. The constructs are curriculum improvement/development, facilitating learning and training, vocational knowledge and expertise, vocational capacity, digital competence, and research and self-development.

In the time of rapid technological and societal changes, curriculum improvement/development presents a special challenge to TVET teachers. That is, curriculum design and instructional planning need to constantly assess and select appropriate and cutting-edge technologies to reflect and meet the changing needs of industry and to enhance student learning and skill training. As an overarching approach, blended learning should guide curriculum and instructional design and development.

This blended learning approach is also applicable to the construct of facilitating learning and training. This can include how to manage a blended learning environment in teaching and training, how to support students in their use of technology in learning and vocational skills development, and how to assess student learning using appropriate technologies and methods.

In terms of vocational knowledge and expertise, this construct embraces two kinds of core capacities for TVET teachers: (1) the capacity to constantly update their own domain knowledge, and (2) the capacity to make best use of technology to engage learners in their acquisition of domain knowledge.

Different from teachers in higher education, TVET teachers play the dual role of facilitating knowledge acquisition and skill training. In skill training, TVET teachers are much like a tradesperson or technician. They need to help students acquire practical skills relevant to their future occupations, often through hands-on learning in a real-world setting. This role requires TVET teachers not only to develop pedagogy for training and supervising students' vocational skills development, but also engage with industry to advance their understanding of industry needs, and update their vocational knowledge and skills accordingly. They also need to collaborate with industry in research, skill training in the workplace, and supervising internship.

In the proposed framework, the level of TVET teachers' digital competence qualitatively exceeds the basic digital literacy possessed by a digital citizen. This construct assumes that in-service TVET teachers have gained their basic digital literacy in their pre-service training such as skills for accessing information through LMS and for using social media. For in-service TVET teachers, they should be able to leverage technology to facilitate student learning and assessments, to solve learning problems, and to innovate and transform their teaching (Almerich et al., 2016; Wagiran et al., 2019a, 2019b). The construct of digital competence in the proposed framework echoes the call of the UNESCO-UNEVOC study (2020a) that TVET teachers and trainers need to build digital skills, acquire knowledge of new technology and equipment, and develop competencies in applying ICT to deliver learner-centered learning and training for the purpose of fostering learners' digital competencies and future oriented skills. The four stages of competency development in this construct align with the four stages of ICT adoption promoted by UNEVOC, namely in emerging, adopting, infusing, and transforming (UNESCO-UNEVOC, 2020b, p. 19).

Lastly, the proposed framework specifies research and self-development as a competency required of today's TVET teachers. This construct addresses the weak culture of research in TVET that has been generally recognized in the literature (Lachlem, 2017; Marope et al., 2015), although research has been one of the three dimensions (with the other two being teaching and management) in the IIOE's (International Institute of Online Education) Teacher ICT Competence Framework developed by ICHEI (International Center for Higher Education Innovation under the auspices of UNESCO). The forever changing demands from today's industry requires TVET teachers to be aware of and constantly informed by new theoretical knowledge and practical developments from industry. Research and self-development is also a process in which TVET teachers reflect upon their teaching practice and innovation through research and publication and develop their agency both individually and in a community of practice. The ability to research and self-develop as a lifelong learner has never been so crucial as it is today. Fortunately, with the aid of technology, this construct can be achieved through a repertoire of resources and a variety of effective means and avenues, be them physical or virtual, online or face to face.

TVET teachers' capacity to use technology in a pedagogically meaningful fashion pervades all of the six constructs in the proposed framework. This is because blended and online learning has become an integral part of today's education. At the same time, technology is also transforming industry and the whole society. The proposed framework also recognizes the multiple roles played by today's TVET teachers. It highlights the dual role of TVET teachers being a content provider and practical skill trainer. The importance of TVET teachers becoming a lifelong learner is also underlined in the framework. We acknowledge that the above proposed framework does not cover every aspect of TVET teachers' competencies needed in the digital age. For example, we excluded some of the so-called soft skills such as teachers' beliefs, values, attitudes and ethics as we focus on digital teaching competencies. We also need to limit the scope of the framework in order to keep it more focused and easier to be used by TVET practitioners. We believe they are equally important and deserve a comprehensive study beyond the focus and scope of the proposed framework.

3.3.2 Rationale for the Stages of the Proposed TVET Teachers' Competency Development

The proposed framework delineates the trajectory of TVET teachers' professional development, progressing from beginner to a competent teacher, and then a proficient teacher to an expert. Different from the five-stage model proposed by Dreyfus and Dreyfus (1986) and Rauner's (2007) five-stage vocational competence development, we excluded the novice stage as we focused on in-service teachers' digital competencies. We believed that in-service teachers were not completely new to technology-supported teaching and training as they should have been trained as teachers in a specific subject area in their preservice training and should have possessed basic digital literacy.

The beginning stage of their competency development can be seen as an awareness raising period. This is a process in which TVET teachers gain a preliminary understanding of the teaching and learning environment that they are going to work in and the competencies required of them to teach in a digital age. It is crucial for them to be conscious of the importance of developing one's professional competencies in an ongoing manner. This can be achieved through teachers' participating in the institution's orientation programs, co-developing curricula with peers, and teaching and training students supervised or with a team. They also need to improve their understanding of domain knowledge and vocational skills through research and regular contact with industry. They may have a sufficient level of digital literacy for accessing online resources for teaching preparation, but they need to develop an understanding of how to apply their digital knowledge to specific instructional design and delivery. They may need guidance and support in every aspect of their professional development at this stage.

Stage two is a transitional stage, in which teachers should have become more competent and independent after adapting to the teaching and learning environment. This stage sees the internalization of their experiences and insights gained in stage one. In terms of curriculum development and delivery, teachers are not only able to integrate and use ICT fluently to support or enable learning and training, they can also use appropriate technology and resources to solve problems arising from their teaching and training. They have acquired a new understanding of domain knowledge and vocational skills needed by industry through engaging with industry. Self-development becomes more self-regulatory and self-paced.

Innovation characterizes the third stage in TVET teachers' professional trajectory. In this stage, teachers have become more proficient and resourceful in curriculum development and facilitation of learning, catalysing the potential of ICT in teaching and training innovation. With the support of ICT and informed by students' learning needs and the demands of industry, teachers begin to venture out of their comfort zone to explore ways to innovate their curricula and improve students' occupational skills development. Research into and reflection on their teaching innovation happen regularly and findings are shared with their peers in communities of practice and/or through publication.

When teachers become an expert in the field in stage four, leadership qualities become the essential competency in the digital age. These qualities can be manifested in their efforts to bring new knowledge, skills, and pedagogies into teaching, learning and training to make them more effective, interactive, enabling, and learner-centred. Such a transformation requires forward thinking that foresees what is needed in future TVET curricula and how ICT can be utilized to prepare students to meet the future needs of industry. Peer mentoring is another leadership quality that expert teachers need to nurture in this stage. Peer mentoring can happen in research projects and publications as well as in teaching innovation.

3.4 TVET Teachers' Competency Indicators and Assessment Instrument

While the above proposed framework outlines the constructs and stages of TVET teachers' competency development, in this section, we first identify three levels of key competency indicators in Sect. 3.4.1 for each of the six competencies contained in the framework in Table 3.1. These indicators define the capabilities and behaviours that a competent TVET teacher should develop in the digital age. Then Sect. 3.4.2 proposes an assessment instrument to help measure these competencies based on the indicators developed in Sect. 3.4.1.

3.4.1 Key Competency Indicators

To further qualify the scope and contents of each competency discussed in Table 3.1, we developed a list of indicators as shown in Table 3.2. They are categorized into three levels, with six first-level indicators, 18 s-level indicators, and 62 third-level indicators.

3.4.2 Assessment Instrument

Based on the competency indicators discussed above, an assessment instrument was proposed (see Table 3.3). It consists of three levels of criteria with six in level 1, 19 in level 2, and 147 in level 3.

Table 3.2 Key indicators for assessing TVET teachers' competency in the digital age

First-level indicators	Second-level indicators	Third-level indicators
A. Curriculum improvement/development	A1. Analysis of industry needs and standards	(a) investigate the needs of industry for subject area/course improvement/development (b) analyze the needs and propose further actions (c) analyze relevant vocational competence standards required by industry (d) adopt/adapt these standards to curriculum improvement/development to meet students' needs
	A2. Analysis of relevant knowledge, skill and professional ethics requirements	(a) Analyze relevant knowledge requirements for the targeted subject area(s)/course(s) (b) Analyze relevant skill requirements for the targeted subject area(s)/course(s) (c) Analyze relevant professional ethics requirements for the targeted subject area(s)/course(s)
	A3. Subject area/course improvement/development	(a) improve/develop subject areas/course objectives (b) improve/develop subject areas/course contents (c) improve/develop subject areas/course structure (d) improve/develop instructional plans (e) improve/develop assessment schemes
	A4. Learning module/project/task improvement/development	(a) improve/develop modules/project/tasks in accordance with relevant vocational competence standards and student needs (b) Specify objectives of each module/project/task (c) Specify procedures for hands-on practice in each module/project/task (d) specify learning outcomes for each module/project/task

(continued)

Table 3.2 (continued)

First-level indicators	Second-level indicators	Third-level indicators
B. Facilitating learning and training	B1. Instructional design	(a) Design learning and training goals (b) Design learning and training activities (c) Design learning and training resources (d) Design learning and training environments (e) Design learning and training evaluation mechanisms
	B2. Teaching and training	(a) Introduce learning/training scenarios/contexts (b) facilitate learning/training activities (c) manage face-to-face/online classrooms (d) maintain student learning and training progress (e) manage hands-on training projects/workshops
	B3. Teaching and learning/training evaluation	(a) Conduct (self) evaluation of curriculum/course (b) Conduct (self) evaluation of teaching (c) Conduct evaluation of learning (d) Conduct evaluation of training
C. Vocational knowledge/expertise	C1. Basic knowledge	(a) Have basic subject matter knowledge/expertise (b) update basic subject matter knowledge/expertise
	C2. Knowledge of new technology	(a) Have professional knowledge of new technology and technological equipment used in industry (b) update professional knowledge of new technology/ technological equipment
D. Vocational capacity	D1. Communication and collaboration skills	(a) Build an institution-industry cooperation/collaboration network (b) participate in services provided by the institution to regional industry

(continued)

Table 3.2 (continued)

First-level indicators	Second-level indicators	Third-level indicators
	D2. Practical vocational skills	(a) Have practical vocational skills in the classroom (b) Have practical vocational skills outside the classroom (on campus) (c) Have off-campus vocational skills (d) foster students' vocational ethics
	D3. Industry service skills	(a) support workplace training in industry (b) provide specialized expertise to support industry
E. Digital competence	E1. Awareness and attitude	(a) Recognize the importance of ICT to TVET (b) Be willing to adopt ICT in teaching (c) Evaluate and reflect on the use of ICT in teaching
	E2. Knowledge and skills	(a) possess basic digital literacy (b) possess Technological Content Knowledge (TCK) (c) possess Technological Pedagogical Knowledge (TPK)
	E3. Application and innovation	(a) Collaborate and communicate via and/or with the support of technology (b) leverage ICT in enhancing teaching, learning, and training (c) leverage ICT in teaching innovation
	E4. Social responsibility	(a) ensure equal opportunities for students to use ICT (b) promote student safe use of ICT (c) promote virtual/online etiquettes

(continued)

Table 3.2 (continued)

First-level indicators	Second-level indicators	Third-level indicators
F. Research and self-development	F1. Research on teaching	(a) integrate research findings into curriculum development and instructional design at both the subject area and course levels (b) Apply research findings to facilitate learning and training (c) innovate teaching and training practice informed by research
	F2. Professional development	(a) Improve professional knowledge and professional competencies in an ongoing manner (b) develop a personal career development plan (c) acquire self-development strategies (d) Participate in continuing professional development activities (e) Organize and participate in teaching and training-related research activities
	F3. Professional ethics	(a) understand and abide by TVET regulations and professional ethics (b) develop and assess student awareness of TVET regulations and professional ethics

3.5 Recommendations for the Use of the Proposed Competency Framework, Indicator, and Assessment Instrument

3.5.1 Informing TVET Teachers' Professional Development at the National Level

First, the proposed framework and indicators and assessment instrument can be used as a reference point when formulating national policies for supporting TVET teachers' professional development. We believe that improving TVET teachers' competencies should go hand in hand with the digital transformation of a country's

Table 3.3 Assessment instrument for TVET teachers' competency in the digital age

First-level criteria	Second-level criteria	Third level criteria
A. Curriculum improvement/development	A1. Analysis of industry needs and standards	(1) Design ways/methods to investigate the needs of industry (2) Analyze the needs of industry (3) Propose action plans (4) Analyze relevant vocational competence standards (5) Adopt/adapt relevant vocational competence standards to meet student needs
	A2. Analysis of relevant vocational knowledge, skills and ethics requirements	(1) Decide on relevant vocational knowledge needed for subject area/course improvement (2) Select relevant skills/expertise needed for subject area/course improvement and development (3) Analyze vocational ethics to impart to students
	A3. Subject area/course improvement/development	(1) Familiar with the objectives of the subject area(s)/course(s) (2) Improve/develop course contents (3) Familiar with the links between courses in a subject area/program (4) Improve/develop subject areas/course structures (5) Improve/develop instructional plans (6) Improve/develop assessment schemes (7) Design hands-on training activities (8) Interpret vocational competence standards (9) Integrate vocational competence standards into curriculum improvement/development

(continued)

Table 3.3 (continued)

First-level criteria	Second-level criteria	Third level criteria
	A4. Module/project/task improvement/development	(1) Improve/develop modules/project/tasks in accordance with relevant vocational competence standards and student needs (2) Develop objectives for each module/project/task (3) Design procedures for hands-on practice in each module/project/task (4) Specify learning outcomes for each module/project/task (5) Design curriculum for modules/projects/tasks (6) Evaluate module/project/task outcomes/effectiveness
B. Facilitating learning and training	B1. Instructional design	(1) Design learning goals (2) Design learning activities (3) Development learning resources (4) Design learning environments (5) Design formative evaluation of learning (6) Design summative evaluation of learning (7) Determine teaching strategies (8) Design training goals (9) Design training activities (10) Determine equipment, tools and materials needed for training activities (11) Design training environments (12) Design training strategies (13) Design diagnostic evaluation of training (14) Design formative evaluation of training (15) Design summative evaluation of training

(continued)

Table 3.3 (continued)

First-level criteria	Second-level criteria	Third level criteria
	B2. Teaching and training	(1) Deliver learning contents effectively (2) Create authentic learning contexts using real/virtual objects, media, and other tools (3) Facilitate learning activities (simulated) in class (4) Manage face-to-face classroom teaching (5) Manage online classroom teaching (6) Motivate students (7) Engage students in learning (8) Support students learning outside class (9) Introduce training contexts (10) Explain training procedures (11) Assemble training materials, equipment, and tools (12) Facilitate skill-based hands-on training activities (13) Solve emerging problems
	B3. Teaching and training evaluation	(1) Implement course evaluation (2) Analyze the feedback from course evaluation (3) Implement teaching evaluation (4) Analyze the feedback from teaching evaluation (5) Implement student learning evaluation (6) Analyze the feedback from student learning evaluation (7) Implement training evaluation (8) Analyze the feedback from training evaluation

(continued)

Table 3.3 (continued)

First-level criteria	Second-level criteria	Third level criteria
C. Vocational knowledge and expertise	C1. Basic vocational knowledge and expertise	(1) Have basic subject matter knowledge and expertise (2) Able to update basic subject matter knowledge and expertise (3) Have relevant industry experiences (4) Update relevant industry experiences
	C2. Knowledge of new technology	(1) Update knowledge of new technology in related fields (2) Use knowledge of new technology in teaching (3) Update knowledge of new technological equipment in industry (4) Use knowledge of new technological equipment in teaching (5) Use knowledge of new technology in training (6) Use knowledge of new technological equipment in training
D. Vocational capacity	D1. Communication and collaboration skills	(1) Communicate with industry (2) Update knowledge of industry developments (3) Collaborate with industry on projects (4) Collaborate with industry on student training (5) Assist local governments in providing services to communities

(continued)

Table 3.3 (continued)

First-level criteria	Second-level criteria	Third level criteria
	D2. Vocational skills	(1) Facilitate hands-on tasks conducted in on-campus training facilities (2) Evaluate the operational status of on-campus training facilities (such as safety risks) (3) Guide students in obtaining qualification certificates (4) Guide students in participating in vocational skill competitions (5) Participate in building off-campus training facilities (6) Supervise student internship (7) Support student internship
	D3. Service to industry	(1) Help industry identify their workplace training needs (2) Help industry develop their workplace training plans according to industry competency standards (3) Help industry conduct their workplace training (4) Help industry evaluate their training effectiveness (5) Collaborate with industry on relevant research and development (R&D) (6) Help promote industry innovations/breakthroughs to society

(continued)

Table 3.3 (continued)

First-level criteria	Second-level criteria	Third level criteria
E. Digital competence	E1. Awareness and attitude	(1) Recognize the importance of ICT to TVET (2) Willing to adopt ICT in teaching and training (3) Willing to evaluate the use of ICT in teaching and training (4) Willing to reflect on the use of ICT in teaching and training (5) Willing to share digital learning resources (6) Aware of the latest developments in ICT (such as big data, cloud computing, Internet of Things, VR/AR, artificial intelligence, 5G network, blockchain, etc.) (7) Aware of the latest developments in technological equipment and tools in industry (8) Aware of the latest developments in technological content knowledge (TCK) (9) Aware of the latest developments in technological pedagogical knowledge (TPK)
	E2. Knowledge and skills	(1) Have basic digital literacy (2) Have technological content knowledge (TCK) (3) Have technological pedagogical knowledge (TPK)

(continued)

Table 3.3 (continued)

First-level criteria	Second-level criteria	Third level criteria
	E3. Application and innovation	(1) Use ICT to develop learning resources (2) Use ICT to facilitate student learning process (3) Use ICT to develop training resources (4) Use ICT to facilitate student training process (5) Use ICT to communicate with students (6) Use ICT to build family-school cooperation (7) Use ICT to collaborate and communicate with colleagues in teaching and research (8) Use ICT to develop contextual/situated learning to integrate theory with practice (9) Use ICT to create hands-on learning opportunities (10) Use ICT to create opportunities for institution-industry cooperation and collaboration (11) Use ICT (e.g., mobile terminals, VR/AR, Internet of Things, 5G) to build a new model of vocational training involving experiment, hands-on practice, and virtual internship (12) Use ICT to enable new learning opportunities such as distance learning, and student self-directed learning outside class (13) Use ICT to enable new training opportunities such as virtual labs, 3D simulations, and robotic assisted training scenarios

(continued)

Table 3.3 (continued)

First-level criteria	Second-level criteria	Third level criteria
	E4. Social responsibility	(1) Ensure that all students have equal access to learning resources, tools, and learning environments (2) Develop students' awareness of cyber security (3) Model online etiquette (4) Model safe use of ICT (5) Model observation of laws and regulations related to the use of ICT
F. Research and self-development	F1. Research on teaching and training	(1) Conduct teaching-related research (2) Integrate research findings into curriculum design (3) Integrate research findings into instructional design (4) Apply research findings to teaching practice (5) Innovate teaching approaches informed by research (6) Conduct training-related research (7) Integrate research findings into training design (8) Apply research findings to training process (9) Innovate training approaches informed by research (10) Conduct research projects (11) Conduct research on vocational education reforms (12) Make recommendations relating to institutional teaching reforms

(continued)

Table 3.3 (continued)

First-level criteria	Second-level criteria	Third level criteria
	F2. Professional development	(1) Self-improve professional knowledge and skills (2) Improve professional knowledge and skills in communities of practice (3) Set goals for self-development (4) Develop strategies for self-development (5) Assess self-development progress (6) Reflect on self-development (7) Reflect on teaching innovation (8) Reflect on student feedback (9) Participate in on-the-job training (10) Able to develop collaborative skills (11) Able to organize teaching related research activities (12) Able to engage in teaching related research activities
	F3. Professional ethics	(1) Familiar with national vocational education laws, regulations, and policies (2) Consciously abide by national vocational education laws, regulations, and policies (3) Comply with professional ethics (4) Comply with relevant industry rules and regulations (5) Explain professional ethics to students (6) Evaluate students' observation of professional ethics

vocational education. In a similar vein, Latchem (2017) argued that digital transformation of TVET "requires the creation of a training ecosystem wherein all of the stakeholders in the internal and external organizational ecosystems agree, collaborate and share resources, information and services" (p. 201). As far as teachers are concerned, their willingness and capability to participate in educational reforms determine the degree of their success. The proposed competency framework and indicators can help examine the current status of TVET teachers' competency level in a country and identify strengths and areas for improvement. Such an analysis can lead to the formulation of well-informed policies and standards for TVET teachers' professional development at the national level. The proposed competency framework can also be used as a reference when improving existing policies and standards for teacher professional development, making them more comprehensive in scope, more specific in content, and more applicable and effective in practice.

Second, the framework and indicators can also provide a reference for the development of national training programs, training courses, and training resources. The reference point can address urgent needs from industry and a country's specific needs for competent TVET teachers. While TVET teacher training workshops, seminars, projects, and other capacity-building activities have been offered by governments around the world, international organizations, non-governmental organizations, and private sectors, many of these training efforts are one-off or lack systematic support and follow-ups (Xiaohan, n.d.).

Third, the framework and indicators can inform the building of national Open Educational Resources (OER) for TVET teachers. Such resources empower teachers with tools and means to adapt and/or reuse readily available resources when designing student learning and training as well as teachers' self-development. Teachers should be provided with a variety of means to access OER. In addition, training how to customize OER for particular learning and training goals should form part of the national professional development programs. Furthermore, a national professional development program should engage teachers to develop their abilities to collect and/or create online teaching resources in local languages to suit local needs. In this regard, attention should be paid to the global campaign for OER and the implementation of the principles of the 2012 Paris OER Declaration.

Fourth, the proposed framework can also help promote the standardization of local teacher training courses. The indicators and criteria statements used in this chapter can facilitate the sharing of local contents across cultures.

3.5.2 Informing TVET Teachers' Professional Development at the Institutional Level

The proposed framework and indicators can be used as a basis for institutions to further develop and formulate policies and standards to promote, guide and support the professional development of their teachers. They can be used to assess the effectiveness of its staff professional development programs and identify gaps to bridge. They can also contribute to the development of an award policy and system (e.g., certificate, micro credential or monetary awards) to encourage and recognize teachers' participation in professional development activities or self-learning. In particular, the proposed four stages of professional development specified in the framework can be referred to when developing or updating key performance indicators and criteria for different levels of staff promotion. Systematic support policies and mechanisms can also be established in accordance with the framework and indicators so as to sustain teachers' agency grow, both individually and in communities of practice. Research shows many institutions in African countries lag behind in meeting the changing needs of teaching in the information age as far as ongoing support for teachers' professional development is concerned.

In terms of informing institutional teacher professional development programs, the proposed framework and indicators can assist institutions in monitoring and improving such programs. A timely understanding of teachers' competency levels can help institutions to evaluate whether their current content, modes and approaches adopted in their teachers' professional development programs meet the requirements of participants' needs in reaching their lifelong development goals. Many institutions lack an integrated approach to teachers' professional development, often with no clear objectives and long-term goals. For example, some institutions focus on teachers' curriculum development ability, and some only train teachers on vocational skills, while others stop at helping teachers develop basic digital literacy without further training on how to integrate ICT to improve, innovate, or enable learning (Subrahmanyam, 2022). The proposed framework and indicators should help institutions develop a systems approach in understanding teachers' needs for upskilling and support so that ongoing interventions can be more targeted and sustained.

Last, but not least, the proposed indicators and assessment instrument can be adapted/adopted to evaluate institution-wide teachers' competency levels in an ongoing manner. The evaluation results can facilitate a constant reappraisal of teachers' competency levels, and in particular, the levels of their technological competence to develop tailored professional development programs and update existing intervention approaches and contents. Such a constant reappraisal is much needed to keep today's TVET current with the fast-changing industry and society. Besides, the four-stage progression suggested by the framework also provides institutional management with an understanding of each individual teacher's personal trajectory from beginner to expert. It also helps institutional management classify teachers into beginners, competent teachers, proficient teachers, and experts so that tailored support can be targeted to each group of teachers.

3.5.3 Guiding Individual Teachers' Self-Development

The proposed assessment instrument is particularly valuable to individual TVET teachers as it can be referred to when assessing their own professional competencies. Used as a self-assessment tool, its three levels of criteria make it easy for individual teachers to ensure a comprehensive coverage and sufficient depth of their self-evaluation. The assessment instrument allows teachers to assess their own specific behaviours and competencies in relation to curriculum development, facilitation of learning and training, vocational knowledge and skills, digital competence, and research and self-development. Such a self-assessment can enable teachers to better understand their levels of competence, professional strengths and weakness, and act accordingly. For example, they would know what OERs to use, which professional development programs to attend, and which communities of practice to join that fit specific needs for further developing their agency.

The four-stage progression contained in the proposed framework also facilitates career goal setting as it lends TVET teachers a holistic view of their professional trajectory. The respective competency levels required of beginner, competent, proficient teacher, and expert help teachers set short term goals for each stage and long-term goals for their whole career. They can adjust their development strategies and tasks according to these goals and eventually become an expert in the field.

References

Almerich, G., Orellana, N., Suárez-Rodríguez, J., Orellana, N., Suárez-Rodríguez, J., & Díaz-García, I. (2016). Teachers' information and communication technology competences: A structural approach. *Computers and Education, 100*, 110–125.

Avis, J., & Orr, K. (2014). The new professionalism: An exploration of vocational education and training teachers in England. In S. Billett, C. Harteis, & H. Gruber (Eds.), *International handbook of research in professional and practice-based learning* (pp.1099–1124). Springer Science+Business Media. https://doi.org/10.1007/978-94-017-8902-8_40

Becker & Spottl. (2019). *Guidelines to vocational disciplines: aligning the Regional TVET teacher standard for ASEAN with relevant economic sectors and occupational fields*. https://asean.org/book/guidelines-to-vocational-disciplines-aligning-the-regional-tvet-teacher-standard-for-asean-with-relevant-economic-sectors-and-occupational-fields/

Becker, M. (2010). Berufliche Fachrichtung Fahrzeugtechnik. In: J.-P. Pahl, & V. Herkner (Hrsg.), *Handbuch Berufliche Fachrichtungen* (S. 461–476). W. Bertelsmann.

Berliner, D. C. (2004). *Expert teachers: Their characteristics, development and accomplishments*. https://www.researchgate.net/publication/255666969_Expert_Teachers_Their_Characteristics_Development_and_Accomplishments

Diao, J.-F., & Yang, J. (2021). Multiple-role perspective on assessing teaching ability: Reframing TVET teachers' competency in the information age. *Journal of Educational Technology Development and Exchange (JETDE), 14*(1), Article 4.

Diep, P. C., & Hartmann, M. (2016). Green skills in vocational teacher education—A model of pedagogical competence for a world of sustainable development. *TVET@Asia, 6*, 1–19.

Dreyfus, H. L., & Dreyfus, S. E. (1986). *Mind over machine*. Free Press.

Fessler, R. (1991). *The teacher career cycle: Understanding and guiding the professional development of teachers*/Ralph Fessler, Judith C. Christensen.
Fuller, F. F. (1969). Concerns of teachers: A developmental characterization. *American Educational Research Journal, 6*, 207–226.
Fuller, F. F., & Bown, O. H. (1975). Becoming a teacher. In K. Ryan (Ed.), *Teacher education (74th Yearbook of the National Society of Education)* (pp. 25–52). University of Chicago Press.
Hall, G. E., & Hord, S. M. (1987). *Change in schools: Facilitating the process*. State University of New York Press.
Hall, G. E., & Hord, S. M. (2006). *Implementing change: Patterns, principles and potholes*. Pearson Education.
Hall, G. E., & Loucks, S. (1978). Teacher concerns as a basis for facilitating and personalizing staff development. *Teachers College Record, 80*(1), 46–58.
Hannafin, M. J., Hill, J. R., Land, S. M., & Lee, E. (2014). Student-centered, open learning environments: Research, theory, and practice. In J. Spector, M. Merrill, J. Elen, & M. Bishop (Eds.), *Handbook of research on educational communications and technology*. Springer. https://doi.org/10.1007/978-1-4614-3185-5_51
Hodges, C., Moore, S., Lockee, B., Trust, T., & Bond, A. (2020). *The difference between emergency remote teaching and online learning*. EDUCAUSE Review. https://er.educause.edu/articles/2020/3/the-difference-between-emergency-remote-teaching-and-online-learning. Accessed July 15, 2021.
Huberman, M. (1992). Teacher development and instructional mastery. In A. Hargreaves & M. Fullan (Eds.), *Understanding teacher development* (pp. 216–241). Longman Publishers.
Jafar, D., Saud, M., Hamid, M., Suhairom, N., Mohd, H., Mohd, H., & Zaid, Y. (2020). TVET teacher professional competency framework in Industry 4.0 era. *Universal Journal of Educational Research, 8*, 1969–1979. https://doi.org/10.13189/ujer.2020.080534
Köpsén, S. (2014). How vocational teachers describe their vocational teacher identity. *Journal of Vocational Education & Training, 66*(2), 194–211. https://doi.org/10.1080/13636820.2014.894554
Latchem, C. (2017). *Using ICTs and blended learning in transforming TVET*. UNESCO-UNEVOC. Retrieved August 27, 2020, from https://unevoc.unesco.org/home/UNESCO%20and%20COL%20Publication%20on%20ICTs%20and%20Blended%20Learning
Liu., & Yin. (2014). The connotation and improvement path of teachers' informatization teaching ability. *Journal of the Chinese Society of Education* (10), 31–36.
London Leadership Academy. (n.d.). *The iceberg model explained*. Retrieved April 5, 2022, from https://www.leadershipbyall.co.uk/wp-content/uploads/2021/04/OW001-Iceberg-Model-Leadership-Academy.pdf
Loucks, S. F., Newlove, B., & Hall, G. E. (1975). *Levels of use of the innovation: A manual for trainers, interviewers, and raters*. Research and Development Center for Teacher Education, University of Texas.
Marope, P. T. M., Chakroun, B., & Holmes, K. P. (2015). *Unleashing the potential: Transforming technical and vocational education and training*. UNESCO. Retrieved May 22, 2016, from http://unesdoc.unesco.org/images/0023/002330/233030e.pdf
Ministry of Education of the PRC. (2020, June 24). *Notice of the ministry of education on issuing the "digital campus specification for vocational colleges"*. http://www.moe.gov.cn/srcsite/A07/zcs_zhgg/202007/t20200702_469886.html
Morrison, G. R. (2010). *Designing effective instruction* (6th Ed.). John Wiley & Sons.
Rauner, F. (2007). Practical knowledge and occupational competence. *European Journal of Vocational Training, 40*(1), 52–66. Cedefop—European Centre for Vocational Training.
Rauner, F. (2021). *Measuring and developing professional competences in COMET: Method manual*. Springer Singapore.
Rutherford, W. L., & Hall, G. (1990). *Concerns of teachers: Revisiting the original theory after twenty years*. Paper presented at the American Educational Research Association (AERA), Boston, USA.

Saunders, R (2012). Assessment of professional development for teachers in the vocational education and training sector: An examination of the concerns based adoption model. *Australian Journal of Education, 56*(2), 182–204.

Subrahmanyam, G. (2022). *Trends mapping study: Digital skills development in TVET teacher training.* Retrieved April 5, 2022, from https://unevoc.unesco.org/pub/trends_mapping_study_digital_skills_development_in_tvet_teacher_training.pdf

The Royal Academy of Engineering in UK (2018). The Career Framework for University Teaching. Retrieved September 6, 2023, from https://teachingframework.com/framework/.

Tyler, M. A., & Dymock, D. (2021). Constructing a professional identity in VET: Teacher perspectives. *Research in Post-Compulsory Education, 26*(1), 1–18. https://doi.org/10.1080/13596748.2021.1873404

UNESCO. (2012a). *2012 Paris OER declaration.* Retrieved April 21, 2022, from http://www.unesco.org/new/fileadmin/MULTIMEDIA/HQ/CI/CI/pdf/Events/English_Paris_OER_Declaration.pdf

UNESCO. (2012b). *The 3rd international congress on technical and vocational education and training.* Retrieved April 5, 2022, from https://uil.unesco.org/lifelong-learning/3rd-international-congress-technical-and-vocational-education-and-training

UNESCO-UNEVOC. (2020a). *Promoting quality in TVET using technology—A practical guide.* Retrieved April 5, 2022, from https://files.eric.ed.gov/fulltext/ED608936.pdf

UNESCO-UNEVOC. (2020b). *Improving the quality of TVET using technology: A practical guide.* UNESCO-UNEVOC International Centre for Technical and Vocational Education and Training, Bonn, Germany

Wagiran, P., Suyanto, W., Sofyan, H., Soenarto, S., & Yudantoko, A. (2019a). Competencies of future vocational teachers: Perspective of in-service teachers and educational experts. *Cakrawala Pendidikan, 38*(2), 388–400.

Wagiran, W., Pardjono, P., Suyanto, W., Sofyan, H., Soenarto, S., & Yudantoko, A. (2019b). Competencies of future vocational teachers: Perspective of in-service teachers and educational experts. *Journal Cakrawala Pendidikan, 38*(2), 387–397. https://doi.org/10.21831/cp.v38i2.25393

Xiaohan, B. (n.d.). *Report on digital transformation of higher education in Arab countries.* Retrieved October 11, 2021, from https://www.ichei.org/Uploads/Download/2021-06-23/60d2e4d98719e.pdf

Xiaohan, B. (n.d.). *Report on digital transformation of higher education in Sub-Saharan Africa.* Retrieved October 11, 2021, from https://www.ichei.org/Uploads/Download/2021-06-07/60bd9222748fd.pdf

Open Access This chapter is licensed under the terms of the Creative Commons Attribution-NonCommercial-NoDerivatives 4.0 International License (http://creativecommons.org/licenses/by-nc-nd/4.0/), which permits any noncommercial use, sharing, distribution and reproduction in any medium or format, as long as you give appropriate credit to the original author(s) and the source, provide a link to the Creative Commons license and indicate if you modified the licensed material. You do not have permission under this license to share adapted material derived from this chapter or parts of it.

The images or other third party material in this chapter are included in the chapter's Creative Commons license, unless indicated otherwise in a credit line to the material. If material is not included in the chapter's Creative Commons license and your intended use is not permitted by statutory regulation or exceeds the permitted use, you will need to obtain permission directly from the copyright holder.

Chapter 4
Strategies for Developing TVET Teachers' Professional Competencies

Qian Zhou, Junfeng Diao, Yuping Wang, Mingxuan Chen, Chengming Yang, Mei Li, Jing Wang, Kaiyu Yi, Xibin Han, Guoqiang Cui, and Tiedao Zhang

4.1 Introduction

This chapter focuses on the strategies adopted in teacher professional development at the national, institutional and individual levels. In Sect. 4.2, we adopted an ecological approach to view the sustainable development of TVET teachers' professional competencies as a dynamic and interactive process facilitated by multi-layered factors working together. It is an integration of and interaction between the efforts made at the national, institutional, and individual levels. These efforts, in turn, determine what strategies, resources, technologies and modes of learning to be adopted. It is the interplay of all these factors that sustains and advances TVET teachers' professional development. In this section, we also propose a teacher training model to facilitate TVET teacher professional development. A review of strategies implemented at each

Q. Zhou (✉) · K. Yi · X. Han
Institute of Education, Tsinghua University, Beijing, China
e-mail: zhouqian@tsinghua.edu.cn

J. Diao
School of Education, Hainan Normal University, Haikou, China

Y. Wang
School of Humanities, Languages and Social Science, Griffith University, Brisbane, Australia

M. Chen · J. Wang
School of Humanities, Jiangnan University, Wuxi, China

C. Yang
Graduate School of Education, Beijing Foreign Studies University, Beijing, China

M. Li · T. Zhang
Beijing Open University, Beijing, China

G. Cui
Villanova Institute for Teaching and Learning, Villanova University, Villanova, PA, USA

© The Author(s) 2024
X. Han et al. (eds.), *Handbook of Technical and Vocational Teacher Professional Development in the Digital Age*, SpringerBriefs in Education,
https://doi.org/10.1007/978-981-99-5937-2_4

4.2 TEVT Teachers' Professional Development: An Ecological Approach and a Training Model

4.2.1 Proposing an Ecological Approach to Promoting TVET Teacher's Professional Development

Theories on adult learning, cognitive apprenticeship, situated learning, learning communities, and lifelong learning have indicated that the professional development of teachers' competencies involve not only teachers' personal efforts for their academic growth, but also supportive efforts from governments and institutions. With a strong focus on teachers' professional development, UNESCO stated in its Incheon Declaration that the educational system needs well-qualified, trained, adequately remunerated, and motivated teachers to ensure quality provision (UNESCO et al., 2015). It stressed the critical role of competent teachers in TVET education in its Strategy for TVET 2016–2021. This includes teachers' role to equip all youth and adults with practical and entrepreneurial competencies to adapt to the ever-changing labor market, which ultimately leads to sustainable societies. UNESCO's strategic plan of teacher development is primarily focused on five areas: (1) monitoring international normative instruments relating to the teaching profession, (2) assisting Member States in developing and evaluating teacher policies and strategies, (3) developing capacities for enhancing the quality of teaching and learning, (4) enhancing the knowledge and evidence base for the implementation and monitoring of the teacher development agenda in Education 2030 Framework for Action, and (5) advocating the advancement of high-quality teaching and learning (UNESCO, n.d.).

To support the sustainable development of TVET teachers' teaching competencies, the handbook proposed an ecological approach to view teacher development as a concerted efforts made at the national, institutional, and individual levels. As illustrated in Fig. 4.1, the three levels of efforts are interconnected and interdependent. Only when working together, teachers' professional development can be sustained.

Figure 4.1 illustrates the relationship between national, institutional, and individual efforts. National efforts including policy and strategy making and financial support provide the necessary macro environment in which both institutional and individual efforts can be nurtured or inhibited. Figure 4.1 also shows that TVET institutions can act as an agent between national policy makers and individual teachers, interpreting national policy orientations on one hand and directly engaging TVET teachers in their professional development on the other. More importantly, an ecological view does not see such interaction as a linear process. Rather, it is relational and multidirectional with all components feeding into one another. For example, ideally, what has been achieved at the institutional and individual levels, through the

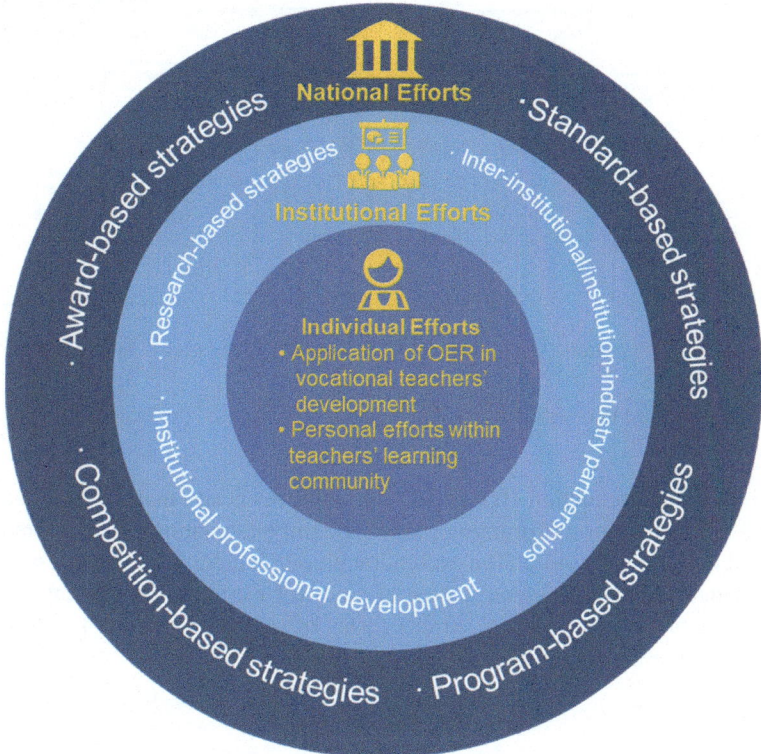

Fig. 4.1 An ecological approach to TVET teachers' professional development

support of national policies and strategies, should, in turn, inform the national policy making process, making national policies and strategies more targeted to institutional and individual changes and needs. Such a cyclic improvement sustains teacher professional development and makes it relevant to industry and student needs.

4.2.2 Proposing a Training Model for TVET Teachers' Competency Development

The conceptual model of training transfer in Human Resource Development (HRD) indicates that learners are only able to transfer their learning into their own practice after going through a dynamic and complex process of training and application (Baldwin & Ford, 1988). This handbook proposed a training model for developing TVET teachers' professional competencies based on the model of transfer. There are three phases in this model, consisting of training design, implementation, and

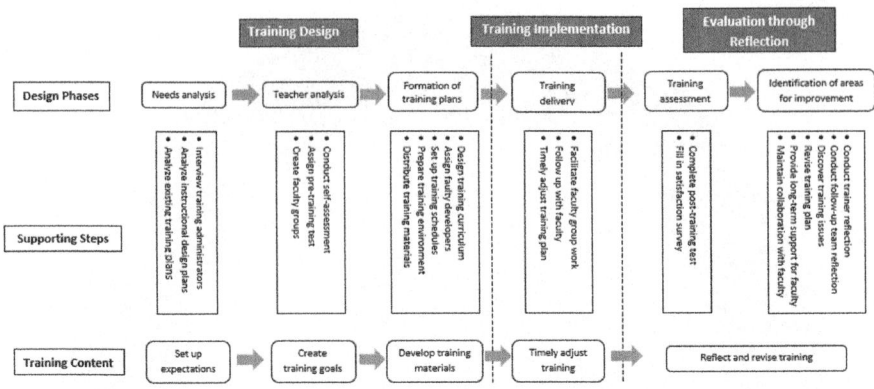

Fig. 4.2 The proposed training model for developing TVET teachers' professional competencies

evaluation through reflection. Training design involves needs analysis, teacher analysis, and the formulation of training plans. The implementation phase refers to the process of delivering training. The evaluation phase includes both the assessment of training outcomes and the identification of areas for further improvement. Such an evaluation is often done through various forms of reflection. Figure 4.2 shows the specific steps within each phase.

4.3 National Efforts for TVET Teachers' Professional Development

Integrating goals of sustainable development of education into national priorities and strategic plans can ensure coherent action at the national level (UNESCO, 2020). Similarly, for TVET, governments need to invest in national efforts to promote its sustainable development. National efforts can be directed to promoting TVET teachers' sustainable development including developing or revising relevant standards and norms, creating training programs, sponsoring teaching competitions, and providing incentives for teacher development (Morgan & White, 2014).

4.3.1 Standard-Based Strategies for Teacher Professional Development

According to Bergmann and Mulkeen (2011), the term "standard" in the context of education means a norm, a requirement, or a quality measure. They argued that a "standard" is an expected quality in the educational system that is commonly referred to, but not mandatory, for all cases. Standard-based strategies for professional development of TVET teachers refer to the issuing of standards that serve as a foundation for TVET teachers' professional development. They will provide guidance for setting goals of teachers' professional development, formulating training curricula, ensuring effective and consistent implementation, and creating evaluation criteria to measure the outcomes and impact of professional development programs. Chapter 3 of this handbook discusses four essential roles of TVET teachers in teachers by profession, vocational practitioner/skill trainers, digital citizens, and lifelong learners. This discussion led to the proposal of a framework for TVET teachers' competency development, which can serve as a reference for developing TVET professional standards.

Many countries have updated their standards of professional competencies for TVET teachers in the information age to maintain the on-going development of teachers' competencies. In 2020, the Association of Southeast Asian Nations (ASEAN) amended its Regional TVET Teachers Standard to encourage positive responses to the opportunities and challenges that digitalization presents in its Member States. The standards serve as a universal tool for recognizing TVET teachers' competencies in the digital age, designing effective and feasible TVET teachers' training plans, and developing reliable measurements for evaluating the performance of TVET teachers.

In Australia, there has been a major push for the use of Information and Communications Technology (ICT) in the delivery of vocational education and training (VET). ICT is considered as part of flexible delivery and a growing shift away from rigid classroom timetables and blocks of time to better meet employer and learner needs (Bound, 2011). ICT is perceived to be able to help teachers become better designers and facilitators of effective teaching and learning. In 2020, the National Center for Vocational Education Research (NCVER) published a study that identified key features of quality teaching in VET and teacher capability frameworks and professional standards in Australia. The study outlined the behaviors, values, skills, and knowledge required for VET teachers at various stages during their careers and the benchmarks to measure their competencies (Misko et al., 2020). Based on the above frameworks and standards, Innovation and Business Skills Australia (IBSA) developed the VET Practitioner Capability Framework to evaluate teacher proficiency by identifying the extent to which the objectives set in teacher performance and professional development plans are met. The recently mandated Certificate IV in Training and Assessment (TAE) update had some deleterious consequences for the VET teaching workforce. Some respondents reported that the additional requirements and costs of regular qualification upgrades were an imposition on providers, especially on small organizations and those relying on volunteer teachers and teachers from equity groups, contributing to teachers exiting the system (Misko et al., 2020).

The European Center for the Development of Vocational Training, the official agency for developing and implementing EU vocational training policies, stated in its report that the professional development of teachers and trainers is one of the priority areas for European cooperation in education and training. The emphasis was kept on the quality of initial education, early career support for new teachers, and on raising the quality of continuing professional development opportunities for teachers, trainers, and other educational personnel. The qualification requirements and training for VET professionals seemed to vary considerably for each country. Therefore, coherent competency frameworks for teachers, trainers, and leaders should be developed to help advance the development of vocational teaching and training in Europe. Such frameworks should define the basic skills and competencies that VET teachers and trainers need to acquire. The development of European Qualification Framework (EQF) and the National Qualification Framework (NQF) are two such examples. They can be seen as a positive move towards effective competency framework building that recognizes the values in developing the professionalism of both individuals and their communities (Frimodt, et al., 2009). The frameworks also included the core activity and competence areas of the VET professions as well as skills and competencies that have emerged more recently such as the role of instructors and trainers in counselling both students and their parents. Furthermore, the frameworks increased the transparency of the profession, making it more socially acceptable and desirable. They also facilitated the development and quality of training in VET where structural support from a training organization did not exist. For example, trainers in small and medium sized enterprises often carry out their training in isolation, without the benefit of the support from a pedagogical leader or counselling services (Volmari et al., 2009).

In 2015, the Ministry of Education of China issued the Professional Standards for Secondary Vocational School Teachers, which provided guidelines for pre-service teacher education, admission, training and evaluation of teaching (Ministry of Education of China, 2013). The Standards for Digital Campus Building for Vocational Schools were published in 2020 which clarified requirements for teachers' information literacy and guided the development of TVET teachers' professional competencies in the digital age.

4.3.2 Program-Based Strategies for Teacher Professional Development

Program-based strategies for teacher development refer to the implementation of national TVET educational reform programs or professional development programs, with the aim to support the continuing development of TVET teachers. Such programs can include training programs for the development of TVET teacher competencies, programs for TVET curriculum and education reform, and programs for promoting innovative teaching in TVET education. Canadian provincial government has been encouraging post-secondary vocational education institutes to engage in applied research in support of business development. Vocational educators are also required to serve on committees and in leadership roles (Hoekstra & Crocker, 2015). With an aim to select outstanding teachers who adopt innovative teaching approaches in all disciplines from all vocational institutions each year, the Chinese Ministry of Education launched the "National TVET Innovative Teaching Team" program in September 2019. The program called for the widespread support of professional development in all vocational schools to encourage continuous development of teachers' professional competence.

4.3.3 Competition-Based Strategies for Teacher Professional Development

Competition-based strategies for teacher development refer to the sponsoring of national competitions to encourage practice and reflection on high-quality vocational teaching, inspire innovations in vocational teaching, and discover exemplary cases of professional development. Since 2010, the Chinese Ministry of Education has held an annual national competition to encourage all vocational institutions to use ICT in teaching, enhance vocational teachers' teaching competence and information literacy, and promote teachers' comprehensive capabilities, professional skills, and innovative teaching and training practice. The competition has evolved into a multi-tiered system of competition at the institutional, provincial/municipal, and national levels, which has significantly contributed to the development of vocational teachers' teaching competence in China. The integration of ICT in teaching has helped vocational teachers enhance their professional competence. Vocational teachers have been encouraged to compete with their counterparts at different levels to employ ICT in their curriculum design and instructional practices to improve learning processes and outcomes (Wang, 2021). Such a competition process has led to the improvement of TVET teachers' professional competencies as they can incorporate best practices learned through the competition into their classrooms. Institutions also support their teachers to participate in the various levels of this national competition. The teachers can, for example, join teams in their own disciplines, observe and learn from other teams, share best practices, and reflect on their current practice and disciplinary requirements. Despite being hampered by the Covid-19 pandemic in 2021, this competition still attracted 240,000 teachers from over 5000 vocational institutions across the country.

4.3.4 Award-Based Strategies for Teacher Professional Development

Award-based strategies of teacher competency development refer to the establishment of national teacher development award scheme which aims to honor teachers who have made significant achievements in educational reform, student development, and teacher professional development. China's National Teaching Achievement Award, for example, is the most prestigious award to recognize efforts on educational reform and best teaching practices across the country. It intends to identify the most original, innovative, and research-informed instructional design and practices that have a significant impact on enhanced teaching and learning outcomes (Ren et al., 2014). The Chinese Ministry of Education made a major adjustment to its National Teaching Achievement Award in 2014, adding the category of "Vocational Education Teaching Achievement Award" to the previous "Higher Education Teaching Achievement Award." This national award, offered every four years, recognizes outstanding teaching achievements in vocational education and forecasts the future direction of vocational education development (Zheng & Huang, 2019). The National Teaching Achievement Award is offered based on three criteria: (1) originality in the context of Chinese TVET, (2) effective implementation for at least two years, and (3) national influence (Zheng, 2019).

In German, the Confederation of German Employers' Associations (BDA) offered the German Employers' Award for Education to honor outstanding institutions for their achievements in educational activities (BDA, 2020). The prize is selected by a panel of educational experts from business, sciences, foundations, and government. It is awarded in the categories of early childhood, school, vocational and tertiary education and is endowed with 10,000 euros each. Although the award is for institutions rather than individual teachers, its selection criteria take into account the participating institution's performance in its teacher participation in professional development, the application of digital media and technology in teaching, and graduates' employment rate. These criteria aim to promote the connection between vocational teaching and industry, and to enhance teachers' teaching competencies and practical vocational skills.

4.4 Institutional Efforts to Promote TVET Teachers' Professional Development

Institutional efforts in supporting TVET teachers' professional development involve not only implementing the national plan for vocational teachers' professional development, but also developing concrete strategies based on local demands for skilled workers, current professional development status, and institution-industry collaboration, and so on. The institutional efforts are critical in bridging the gap between national initiatives and individual faculty development. Generally speaking, vocational institutions offer a variety of training opportunities to support and guide their teachers' ongoing professional development. Those institutional efforts include

inter-institutional or collaborative training programs organized by vocational institutions and industry. Unlike government-supported training, institutional programs are typically organized by school administrators, who maintain a better control and flexibility in selecting training teams, creating training content, and assessing training performance. The advantage of institution-sponsored professional development is that it allows the tracking of teachers' development since their onboarding and can therefore, timely and effectively adjust trainings based on the specific needs of the teachers.

4.4.1 Inter-institutional/institution-Industry Partnerships

TVET teachers' multiple roles (see discussion in Sect. 3.2.1 in Chap. 3) require that their professional development should not only focus on the continuing improvement of their domain knowledge and expertise in the subject matter, but also update occupational knowledge and practical skills. Periodically updating content used in professional development is critical for responding to new demands brought about by digital transformation in the industry.

In Singapore, Nanyang Polytechnic (NYP) developed a "No Shelf Life" approach to promote a borderless culture and environment for TVET teacher development (NYP, 2005). It is important to embrace the notion of lifelong learning as the shelf life of skills is diminishing due to new development of technology and ever-changing industry needs. NYP has been sending their teachers to top universities abroad for further study and encouraging engagement in industrial projects. Rotating every 1 or 2 years, 20% of their academic staff must participate in industry Research and Development (R&D) projects. The department heads are in charge of faculty development in their departments, determining training plans for technology adoption, and improvement of teaching competencies, and R&D skills so that teachers are prepared to adjust or advance as curricula change. Their teachers must have at least a bachelor's degree and 3–5 years of work experience in industry. They bring a wealth of knowledge, work experience, and collaborative relationships and projects with industries. These teachers with both extensive theoretical knowledge and practical industry work experience promote the implementation of the "teaching factory" concept. Teachers in NYP serve in a variety of capacities as teachers, engineers, administrators, and mangers. A significant aspect of the "teaching factory" is carrying out R&D projects in collaboration with industry, integrating teaching practices with industry R&D projects. Thanks to the collaborative partnership, teachers can communicate with industry and students have the opportunity to participate in industry R&D projects. Collaborating with industry also helps enhance teachers' understanding of the cutting-edge technology in industry, push administrators and teachers to proactively prepare for new curricula, enable rapid design and development of new courses, and develop teachers' professional competencies and research capabilities (Xu, 2017).

In higher vocational education in Slovenia, curricula are designed and delivered by both lecturers and in-company trainers. Lecturers must have a qualification including a relevant master's degree, three years of work experience, and relevant professional achievements such as experience on an examination committee and a (co-)author of an education program or textbook. Teachers are employed by vocational institutions and paid by the education ministry. Based on the number of learners enrolled in the programs, they can be employed on a full-time or part-time basis. They can be promoted to supervisors, advisors, or institutional heads. Promotions are usually proposed by the school council. The education ministry evaluates proposals and awards promotions/professional titles. These titles, once acquired, are permanent. Teachers are entitled to 15 days of Continuing Professional Development (CPD) every three years. CPD is not compulsory. The education ministry and the employer/school both contribute a portion of the funding of CPD. Schools can also collaborate with public or private providers of CPD in offering CPD programs to faculty. In-company mentor training is also promoted primarily through the European Social Fund (ESF) projects. The project provides 50 h of free training for mentors attending upper secondary courses, and 60 h for mentors participating in work-based learning (WBL) in higher vocational courses. Those courses cover topics such as pedagogy/andragogy, youth psychology, communication skills, workplace health and safety, and learning monitoring and assessment (CEDEFOP, 2021).

In Australia, vocational teachers, trainers, and assessors are educated and trained through the TAE10 Package, which consists of a number of relevant certifications (10 programs). VET staff working in international education can earn a Graduate Certificate through the TAE 10 package, complimented by a Diploma in the same area. Graduate Certificate and Diploma certifications are available from the TAE 10 package for staff working in learning management (Hugh & Pam, 2013).

4.4.2 Institutional Professional Development

Institutional professional development opportunities are offered in alignment with national and regional initiatives for educational reform and the development of vocational teachers in China. Based on the analysis of institutional professional development efforts, many workshops, seminars, guest lectures, and teaching demonstrations have been offered at different institutions to support their teaching reforms and teachers' professional development while integrating internal and external training resources (Diao & Yang, 2021).

Training programs at various institutions in China have been well-received due to its flexible delivery formats (Jing, 2017). Special attention should also be taken while inviting specialists for training and sending faculty to practice in industry. In comparison to higher education, vocational education involves stronger technical and practical skills, which requires extensive institution-industry collaboration by inviting industrial technical specialists from industry to support vocational teachers' professional development. Those experts, who come from the industry front lines, are intimately familiar with industry needs, workflow, key procedures, development trends, and new standards expected of employees and can thus, help vocational institutions keep their instructional content up to date.

Vocational institutions can conduct research in their partner industries, participate actively in their everyday activities, study the most up-to-date industrial technology, so as to integrate such knowledge into their teaching. Practical experience gained from industry can assist vocational teachers in improving their hands-on skills and learning how to use various tools and technological equipment (Liang, 2014).

When designing training plans and programs, vocational institutions should pay attention to teachers' long-term development. The achievements of professional development gained through training should be reflected in daily teaching practice beyond the training phase. Most of the current professional development training programs are delivered as one-off, isolated events, without explicit alignment between different programs as far as training objectives and program activities are concerned (Diao et al., 2021). Therefore, building a comprehensive training system to provide systematic support for sustainable development of vocational teachers is crucial. Such a system is particularly needed today as new concepts, methods, and technologies are emerging almost every day in a time of digital transformation. The outbreak of the pandemic has brought attention to the unpredictability of societal changes that can disrupt our education system without a warning. Training in vocational education should be constantly updated to support teachers' emerging needs. In addition, vocational institutions should also consider revision of training content and delivery approaches to their training programs. The integration of ICT in vocational education has enabled many innovative training contents and delivery approaches for teacher development. Professional development can now be delivered anytime anywhere due to the advancement of online learning. Lastly, establishing centers for faculty development can promote further development. Targeting on specific challenges teachers encounter in different phases in their career development, the teaching centers can organize customized training to advance faculty's professional competencies in terms of theoretical perceptions and pedagogical approaches and practices (Diao et al., 2021).

4.4.3 Research-Based Strategies for Promotion of Teachers' Competencies

From an action research perspective, another important approach to promoting teachers' professional development is to encourage them to participate in research-based projects relating to institutional initiatives on educational reform and teacher development. Participation in those initiatives can lead to an in-depth understanding of vocational faculty's own teaching practices and an increased awareness of responsibilities, thus contributing to better learning outcomes. In 2015, the Ministry of Education of China released a policy on promoting educational reform and learner development in vocational education. According to the policy, teaching reform in vocational education should be informed by teaching related research. Vocational institutions should establish special projects to research on key issues and challenges in educational reform and learner needs. The policy also encourages joint research efforts from both vocational institutions and industry (Tan, 2018). Research projects on vocational education reform should focus on problems experienced during the reform process with theoretical and practical implications. It was stressed in the policy that these research projects should be guided by theories relating to education reform, with a strong emphasis on project outcomes being highly facilitative of teaching practice.

4.5 Teachers' Individual Efforts for Professional Development

As an external driving factor, the national and institutional efforts provide guidance for the development of pedagogy, delivery approaches, and evaluation of vocational teacher development. However, the sustainable development of vocational teachers' competencies depends more on the individual efforts, driven by their career commitment and lifelong learning beliefs, to develop themselves through various learning opportunities. The development of information technology has empowered teachers' self-development potential and provided many opportunities for teachers' self-development such as via Open Educational Resources (OER) and the building of teachers' learning communities.

4.5.1 The Use of OER in Vocational Teachers' Self-development

The term Open Educational Resources (OER) first came into use at a UNESCO conference in 2002 to embrace concepts such as "open courses" and "open teaching–learning resources." Organization for Economic Co-operation and Development (OECD) later defined OER as "open educational resources are digitized materials offered freely and openly for educators, students and self-learners to use and reuse for teaching, learning and research" (OECD, 2007). Hewlett Foundation's definition of OER has been widely recognized and they defined OER as "teaching, learning, and research resources that reside in the public domain or have been released under an intellectual property license that permits their free use or re-purposing by others. Open educational resources include full courses, course materials, modules, textbooks, streaming videos, tests, software, and any other tools, materials, or techniques used to support access to knowledge" (Atkins et al., 2007). The General Conference of UNESCO made the following recommendation on OER at its 40th session in November 2019. OER are "learning, teaching and research materials in any format and medium that reside in the public domain or are under copyright that have been released under an open license, that permit no-cost access, re-use, re-purpose, adaptation and redistribution by others" (http://portal.unesco.org/en/ev.php-URL_ID=49556&URL_DO=DO_TOPIC&URL_SECTION=201.html).

The OER movement has empowered researchers and educators to become more innovative in their teaching and learning, through its openness and flexibility (Sandanayake, 2019). The use of OER can provide access to various resources and assist faculty to create their own self-sustained online repository, as well as bringing together resources from academia and industry. UNESCO (2019) also stressed the importance of adopting OER and they stated that in-service and pre-service teachers should have the capability of accessing, using, adapting, creating, and sharing OERs. Teachers should be able to find and evaluate appropriate OERs that suit their specific languages, disciplines, subject-matters, educational levels, students' demography, and more (Perifanou & Economides, 2021). For vocational teachers, they need to develop expertise and skills to better take advantage of existing OERs for improving their teaching as well as for their own professional development.

4.5.2 *Personal Efforts Within Teachers' Learning Communities*

Learning communities are an important approach to promoting teacher development at vocational institutions. They are a valuable venue to foster teacher collaboration, share teaching innovations, and drive teaching excellence. For a long time, teachers' professional growth and development have been primarily dependent on the individual efforts of teachers. However, professional development cannot rely solely on individual efforts as learning involves other social factors. Therefore, it becomes crucial to build a cooperative and collaborative learning platform to promote teachers' growth and address the challenges of individual learning such as social isolation (Yang, 2017).

A learning community in TVET is a group consisting largely of vocational teachers. With a purpose to promote teacher professional development, student growth, and educational reform, the learning-centered community creates a diversely multi-channel, collaborative, and supportive network among teachers, vocational institutions, industries, and societies. Theories on social learning, cooperation and collaboration, learning organization, constructivism, and team coordination have provided the theoretical bases for such communities.

In view of the above characteristics of learning communities, this handbook makes the following four recommendations for developing learning communities in TVET (Wang, 2007). First, a learning community should be led by prominent teachers. Vocational teachers' learning communities are a voluntary learning group to share and discuss teaching and learning issues and practices. With a goal to discuss/resolve academic challenges confronted in teaching practice, this learning community is non-administrative and complementary to the conventional teaching groups who meet to prepare for teaching, conduct research, or develop curricula. The learning community selects its leaders based on their academic influence, and the community is effectively governed through shared responsibilities.

Second, best practices in teaching and research should be shared within the community via a variety of activities. As part of the teacher development initiatives, the learning community sees that front-line teachers within the learning community propose topics or issues for discussion or advice. Discussions within the community are often facilitated by the community leader with other community members participating voluntarily. This is also a process in which community leaders improve their academic knowledge and capacity while discussing solutions or providing advice/guidance. Eventually the collective wisdom from the learning community contributes to advice or suggested solutions.

Third, the collective wisdom of the learning community should facilitate the integration of research into teaching and vice versa. The learning community, led by prominent teachers and industry experts, can provide directions for teachers' professional development, and ensure that teaching and research complement each other. The learning communities discuss, analyze, and investigate real-world problems relating to market demands and market prospects. Results from their analyses are shared by industry experts, resulting in new knowledge, solutions, technologies, or concepts developed within the community.

Fourth, learning communities can contribute to the development of an institutional teacher training system that integrates teaching, research, and continuing development. Such a system should place an emphasis on strengthening teaching and research incentives, performance evaluation, and communication to maximize the use of institutional teaching and research resources. The support system ultimately leads to the effective development of TVET teachers' learning communities.

4.6 Concluding Remarks

In this chapter, we adopted an ecological approach to understanding the dynamic and interactive nature of teacher professional development. Guided by this approach, our review of the efforts made at the national/international, institutional and individual levels reveals that teacher professional development is multifaceted with different components constantly interacting with one another. It has been the interplay of these components that motivates the constant growth of TVET teachers' professional competencies. Furthermore, the discussion throughout this chapter also indicates that in the time of digital transformation, technology plays a crucial intermediating role in driving professional development for TVET teachers forward.

References

Atkins, D. E., Brown, J. S., & Hammond, A. L. (2007). *A review of the open educational resources (OER) movement: Achievements, challenges, and new opportunities (Report to the William and Flora Hewlett Foundation)*. William and Flora Hewlett Foundation.
Baldwin, T. T. & Ford, J. K. (1988). Transfer of training: A review and directions for future research. *Personnel Psychology, 41*(65).
BDA. (2020). *The German Employer award for education [EB/OL]* [2022-01-20]. https://arbeitgeber.de/en/deutsche-arbeitgeberpreis-fuer-bildung-fuer-vier-einrichtungen/
Bergmann, H., & Mulkeen, A. (2011). *Standards for quality in education. Experiences from different countries and lessons learnt*. Deutsche Gesellschaft für Internationale Zusammenarbeit (GIZ) GmbH.
Bound, H. (2011). Vocational education and training teacher professional development: Tensions and context. *Studies in Continuing Education, 33*(2), 107–119. https://doi.org/10.1080/0158037X.2011.554176
CEDEFOP. (2021). *Vocational education and training in Slovenia: Short description*. Publications Office of the European Union. https://doi.org/10.2801/195991
Diao, J., Han, X., & Zhang, Y. (2021). An analysis on developing teacher's ICT skills during the pandemic—A case study based on 28 vocational institutions. *E-Education Research, 42*(01), 115–121.
Diao, J., & Yang, J. (2021). Multiple-role perspective on assessing teaching ability: reframing TVET teachers' competency in the information age. *Journal of Educational Technology Development and Exchange. 14*(1), 57–77.
Frimodt, R. H., Volmari, K., & Helakorpi, S. (2009). *Competence framework for VET professions: Handbook for practioners*.https://www.cedefop.europa.eu/files/111332_Competence_framework_for_VET_professions.pdf
Hoekstra, A., & Crocker, J. R. (2015). Design, implementation, and evaluation of an eportfolio approach to support faculty development in vocational education. *Studies in Educational Evaluation, 46*, 61–73.
Hugh, G., & Pam, E. (2013). *VET teacher, trainer and assessor capabilities, qualifications and development: Issues and options*. Retrieved November 20, 2021, from http://hdl.voced.edu.au/10707/345486
Jing, T. (2017). *A case study on school-based training of vocational teachers*. Shenyang Normal University.
Liang, A. (2014). *A study on the path of professional development of teachers in secondary vocational schools* (pp. 136–137). Southwest Jiaotong University Press.
Ministry of Education of China. (2013). *Notice on the issuance of "Professional Standards for Teachers in Secondary Vocational Schools*. http://www.gov.cn/gongbao/content/2013/content_2547146.htm
Misko, J., Guthrie, H., & Waters, M. (2020, September 15). *Building capability and quality in VET teaching: Opportunities and challenges*. Retrieved November 13, 2021, from https://www.ncver.edu.au/research-and-statistics/publications/all-publications/building-capability-and-quality-in-vet-teaching-opportunities-and-challenges
Morgan, W. J., & White, I. (2014). Education for global development: Reconciling society, state, and market. *Weiterbildung, 1*, 38–41.
NYP (2005). *"No Shelf Life" in a borderless culture at Nanyang Polytechnic*. https://www.enterprisesg.gov.sg/-/media/esg/files/quality-and-standards/business-excellence/pea_nyp_2005_summary_report.pdf?la=en
OECD. (2007). *Giving knowledge for free: The emergence of open educational resources*. Author. Retrieved from http://www.oecd.org/dataoecd/35/7/38654317.pdf
Perifanou, M., & Economides, A. (2021). Designing teachers' training on adopting OERs in their teaching. Retrieved October 30, 2021, from http://end-educationconference.org/wp-content/uploads/2021/07/2021end002.pdf

Ren, J., Wang, Q., Wang, Y., & Zhang, J. (2014). An analysis of national vocational education teaching achievement awards in 2014. *Chinese Association of Higher Education, 2014*(12), 62–66.

Sandanayake, T. C. (2019). Promoting open educational resources-based blended learning. *Int J Educ Technol High Educ 16*(3). https://doi.org/10.1186/s41239-019-0133-6

Tan, Y. (2018). Research on issues in applying and implementation of vocational educational reform funding. *Vocational Education in China, 2018*(01), 64–67+89.

UNESCO. (n.d.). *Teachers*. Retrieved October 26, 2021, from https://en.unesco.org/themes/teachers

UNESCO, Ministry of Education Republic of Korea, UNDP, UNFPA, UNICEF, UN Woman, UNHCRr, & World Bank Group. (2015). *Incheon Declaration: Education 2030: Towards Inclusive and equitable quality education and lifelong learning for all*. https://unesdoc.unesco.org/ark:/48223/pf0000233137

UNESCO. (2019). *Recommendation on open educational resources (OER)*. https://www.unesco.org/en/legalaffairs/recommendation-open-educational-resources-oer

UNESCO. (2020). *Education for sustainable development: A roadmap [R/OL]* [2020-10-11]. https://unesdoc.unesco.org/ark:/48223/pf0000374802

Volmari, K., Helakorpi, S., & Frimodt, R. (2009). *Competence framework for VET professions. Handbook for practitioners*. Retrieved November 20, 2021, from https://www.researchgate.net/publication/305683916_COMPETENCE_FRAMEWORK_FOR_VET_PROFESSIONS_Handbook_for_practitioners

Wang, L. (2021). The impact of national vocational teaching competition on teacher development—A case from Lanzhou petrochemical college of vocational technology. *China Training, 2021*(04), 37–38.

Wang, Z. (2007). Construction of teachers' community in the context of teacher professionalization. *Continuing Education Research, 2007*(02), 62–63.

Xu, H. (2017). *Professional development of vocational teachers: The dilemma and solutions* (pp. 112–113). Shanhai Jiao Tao University Press.

Yang, X. (2017). Problems and reconstruction options in building vocational institutions' learning community. *Vocational & Technical Education Forum, 2017*(14), 9–12.

Zheng, Y. (2019). A reflection on national vocational education teaching achievement awards—Cases from Jiansu and Zhejiang Provinces. *Jiangsu Education, 2019*(52), 8–11.

Zheng, Y., & Huang, H. (2019). An analysis on national vocational education teaching achievement awards during the past two years. *Chinese Association of Higher Education, 2019*(02), 67–72.

Open Access This chapter is licensed under the terms of the Creative Commons Attribution-NonCommercial-NoDerivatives 4.0 International License (http://creativecommons.org/licenses/by-nc-nd/4.0/), which permits any noncommercial use, sharing, distribution and reproduction in any medium or format, as long as you give appropriate credit to the original author(s) and the source, provide a link to the Creative Commons license and indicate if you modified the licensed material. You do not have permission under this license to share adapted material derived from this chapter or parts of it.

The images or other third party material in this chapter are included in the chapter's Creative Commons license, unless indicated otherwise in a credit line to the material. If material is not included in the chapter's Creative Commons license and your intended use is not permitted by statutory regulation or exceeds the permitted use, you will need to obtain permission directly from the copyright holder.

Chapter 5
Exemplars of Good Practice

Tiedao Zhang, Qian Zhou, Chengming Yang, Xiaojing Bai, Xibin Han, Guoqiang Cui, and Yuping Wang

5.1 Case 1 The Annual National Competition for Promoting Teaching Competencies of TVET Teachers: A Case from China[1]

5.1.1 Background

The Ministry of Education of China launched the First National Competition for Promoting Competencies of TVET Teachers in 2010, with an intention to enhance the teaching and learning performance among all vocational schools and colleges across the country and to disseminate best teaching practices both in the classroom and in online mode. With annual operation and constant improvements over the past ten years, the competition has now become a most effective mechanism for upgrading the teaching competencies of vocational teachers, both for face-to-face and online teaching practices and vocational skill training.

---

[1] The draft material was prepared by Li Meng, a Ph.D. student at Tsinghua University.

T. Zhang (✉) · X. Bai
Beijing Open University, Beijing, China
e-mail: drtdzhang@163.com

Q. Zhou · X. Han
Institute of Education, Tsinghua University, Beijing, China

C. Yang
Graduate School of Education, Beijing Foreign Studies University, Beijing, China

G. Cui
Villanova Institute for Teaching and Learning, Villanova University, Villanova, PA, USA

Y. Wang
School of Humanities, Languages and Social Science, Griffith University, Brisbane, Australia

© The Author(s) 2024
X. Han et al. (eds.), *Handbook of Technical and Vocational Teacher Professional Development in the Digital Age*, SpringerBriefs in Education,
https://doi.org/10.1007/978-981-99-5937-2_5

The number of entries for the competition has been increasing each year. There were 16,900 in 2019 but the number increased to 58,100 in 2021. Because of the constant lock-downs due to the COVID pandemic since 2020, classroom instruction has been changed to online or blended delivery mode. In 2021, there were 240,000 vocational teachers participating in institutional level competitions, and 881 best lessons were nominated for the national competition.

5.1.2 The Competition Process

The objectives of this national competition are to showcase innovative performances with a particular focus on instructional design, implementation of innovative practice facilitated by technology, the evaluation of student learning outcomes as well as teachers' reflections for further improvement. Participating teachers are selected at the institutional and municipal/provincial levels first and only the winners are qualified for the national competition.

In recent years, the national competition has been geared towards identifying the best practices in employing digital technologies to innovate teaching and learning. Such practices should provide examples of technology-assisted and/or enabled pedagogical approaches and innovative practices and outcomes, which serve as a useful reference for all TVET practitioners. The competition covers two categories of entries, namely foundation courses and specialized courses. Each of the categories is assessed in five areas: namely, objectives and contexts, contents and approaches, implementation and impacts, pedagogical competence and innovative impact.

- Assessment criteria for college foundation courses

Foundation courses are assessed with such criteria as being essential contents, learner-centered approaches and wider applicability. Innovative practices are assessed with specific attention on setting objectives according to students' needs (20%), content design and delivery through blended approaches (20%), implementation processes and learning outcomes (30%), teaching competence (15%) as well as innovativeness (15%).

- Assessment criteria for discipline-specific (specialized skills) courses

The competition specifies that all the disciplinary-specific courses and curriculum modules need to be relevantly designed in accordance with workplace needs, delivered through hands-on learning, project-based learning, case studies, and situational learning. In support of these approaches, guidebooks and manuals are encouraged to be developed together with digital resources. In regard to vocational skill training and practices, a variety of cutting-edge technologies should be exploited such as virtual simulation, virtual reality and augmented reality to facilitate task-based learning in a real-life like context and develop students' analytical and problem-solving skills.

5.1.3 Implementation and Impacts of the Competition

Before 2021, this national event had been held at a different capital city in China each year. All participating teacher needed to present their entries in front of an assessment panel at the designated venue. In 2021, to mitigate the widespread impacts of the COVID pandemic, the competition adopted some new modalities to ensure its smooth operation. These include holding the competition in both physical and online modes. The physical mode allowed participants to showcase their entry lessons in their own classrooms with their students, instead of a panel evaluation expert team. This alleviated the burden of traveling and possible infection during COVID for the participating teachers. The process of the presentation was recorded and submitted online for assessment by an online panel. This blended mode of participation proved highly successful as the competition attracted much more participants than before.

Thanks to the wide coverage and ease of access of the online participation mode, 220,000 vocational teachers took part in the 2021 competition, representing 18.3% of the total number of TVET teachers in China. Besides, for the first time, the entries covered all the courses across the 19 disciplinary areas.

As a national level annual event for the promotion of vocational teaching competencies particularly for digital instruction, the competition is now jointly organized by the Ministry of Education as well as other employment-related government agencies. Thousands of entry courses have been designed and constructed, making full use of online platforms, new digital technologies and innovative blended instructional approaches to engage learners in integrated learning environment. To ensure the efficient operation and accountability of the competition, different expert committees have been formed to work as a consortium.

This annual national competition has become a massive training and best practice dissemination mechanism for promoting the use of new technologies to innovate TVET teaching and provide quality learning experiences for students. It has also become an important venue for TVET teachers' professional development. To TVET teachers as well as colleges, such an exercise has demonstrated a cost-effective drive for capacity building.

5.2 Case 2 Government Strategies for Sustaining TVET Teachers' Professional Development in the Industry 4.0 Ara: A Case from Germany[2]

In 2011, the German Government published its "High Tech Strategy" at the Hanover Industrial Fair and introduced the concept of Industry 4.0 for the first time (BMBF, 2014). In 2013, the German government launched the "Industry 4.0 platform," which

---

[2] This case is based on the materials provided by Yang ChengMing, a postdoctor at Qinghua University. Source of this case: Breiter et al. (2017).

brought together various industrial associations and companies to form a massive government-led network to promote Industry 4.0 (Federal Ministry for Economic Affairs and Climate Action, n.d.). These developments gave birth to the concept of Vocational Education and Training "4.0," which explored the prospects of developing future workforce that met the requirement of Industry 4.0. To achieve the goals of Vocational Education and Training "4.0", vocational teachers must improve their ability to use digital media and technology in their teaching.

The German Government, in collaboration with vocational institutions and enterprises, has promoted the development of vocational teacher's professional competencies through various strategies including developing standards of vocational teachers' competencies for meeting the demands of the digital age, establishing a digital media competency framework for corporate trainers, building an online platform to continuously develop corporate trainers, and financially supporting vocational teachers' competency development.

5.2.1 Setting Competency Standards for Vocational Teachers in the Digital Age

Bundesinstit fur Berufsbildung (BIBB), ithe Federal Institute for Vocational Education and Training, issued an "Education Strategy for a Digital Knowledge Society" in October 2016, which placed a new emphasis on educational digitalization and required vocational teachers to integrate digital technology into their curriculum design and delivery. The German Standing Conference of Ministers of Education and Cultural Affairs (KMK) also issued "Education in the Digital World" in December 2016, which stated that the development of vocational teachers was a top priority in the digitalization of vocational education. Furthermore, this document also set criteria and standards for vocational teachers' competencies, providing a useful reference for TVET teachers' digital competence development in different phases of their professional life. These policies and criteria led to the KMK's proposal of the following prerequisites for future TVET teachers to be technologically and pedagogically competent:

- The ability to develop a diverse range of digital competencies. This involves collaboration, team networking, instructional management, effective integration of digital media into the classroom, and secure handling of educational data.
- The knowledge of the impact of media and digitalization on students and the ability to develop an effective media-assisted teaching plan to promote students' digital media skills.
- Promoting the effective and creative use of digital tools in personalized and collaborative learning in response to the learner's needs and preferences.
- Providing personalized support for individual and group learning both in and outside the classroom.

- Selecting relevant instructional materials and applications for individual and group projects based on appropriate vocational education quality criteria.
- Supporting students' media-assisted learning and developing their digital media production skills.
- Creating and implementing learning projects based on professional experience in collaboration with internal and external instructors and experts.
- Analyzing current educational research studies in the digital environment and seeking further education opportunities.
- Applying knowledge of copyright, data protection and safety, and youth media protection in building a safe learning environment. Promoting students' conscious and rational use of media and data based on their awareness of the consequences of their behaviors.

5.2.2 Developing a Model for Developing Corporate Trainers' Media-Pedagogical Competence

The digital transformation of industry poses new challenges for corporate trainers as they must be able to provide training based on the new developments and characteristics of industry needs. This requires corporate trainers to understand and assess the functionality and potential of digital media including learning software and platforms, social media, digital tools, applications, e-books, and more. They should also have the ability to critically evaluate other factors such as digital media providers, potentials and hazards, and developmental trends before deciding on the adoption of digital media in vocational education and training (Breiter et al., 2017).

In view of these challenges, BIBB conducted a research project called "Digital media in vocational education and training" e.g., media appropriation and media use in the everyday practice of company-based training staff," to investigate challenges faced by company-based training staff. The research proposed three core questions including: (1) How do company-based training staff select digital media for initial and continuing training practice? (2) How are digital media integrated into initial and continuing training processes? and (3) What support do company-based training staff need to integrate digital media into training in the best possible way? Those questions were formulated to clarify and confirm media-pedagogical competencies that are needed in corporate training (Breiter et al., 2017).

Based on their findings, BIBB proposed a media-pedagogical competence model for corporate trainers. The model is composed of three components, "media didactics," "media education," and "media integration," which are all interrelated. Media didactic competence involves identifying and selecting visualizations, simulations, and animations for training. Media education competence refers to the ethical use of media such as developing and implementing appropriate procedures to combat cyberbullying. Media integration competence includes the capability to integrate various resources to achieve learning goals such as collaborating with the working council and data representatives to develop a learning platform.

To help corporate trainers achieve these competencies, BIBB also proposed an acquisition model to illustrate the process of acquiring these competencies. This model specifies that * MERGEFORMAT the individual process elements of "conditions" (recognizing and taking into account), "approaches" (identifying and assessing) "existing examples" (identifying and assessing) and "own provision" (developing, implementing and evaluating) are all interlinked and cyclic, indicating the propensity of continuous development of media-pedagogical competencies. Additionally, such an acquisition process can be applied to the three types of media-pedagogical competence suggested in the media-pedagogical competence model proposed by Breiter et al. (2017). For example, to develop the media didactics competence, it is important to first recognize its conditions, and then to identify approaches of implementation. This should be followed by assessing existing examples before developing a company's own provision of media (Tulodziecki et al., 2019).

5.2.3 Creating an Online Platform for the Continuing Development of Corporate Trainers

To achieve the sustainable development of corporate trainers' competencies, BIBB launched foraus.de, an online portal that delivers high-quality training and support for corporate trainers in November 2014. The portal offers a wide range of online services, including essential information on how to organize company-based training on a regular basis. The services available via the portal support initial and ongoing training practices and contribute to the continuing development of vocational education and training. The portal currently has around 11,500 registered members and hosts the largest community of trainers in Germany.

5.2.4 Financially Supporting the Development of TVET Teachers' Competencies

Another typical aspect of German government efforts in improving vocational teachers' competencies in the digital age is increased financial support for various initiatives relating to ICT adoption in vocational education and the training of corporate trainers such as the development of Open Educational Resources (OER), and national training programs. In 2016, the German Federal Ministry of Education and Research launched the "Vocational Education and Training 4.0" Framework Initiative. Accompanied with funding support, the initiative's goal is to upgrade training equipment and promote the use of digital media in vocational education and training. One of the supported programs, "Digital Media in Vocational Education: The Application of Digital Media in Vocational Education," received a grant of €152 million for the period 2012–2019. The program aided in the development of digital learning and teaching curricula to meet industry needs such as mobile learning and Web-based teaching. Besides, the program also assisted the development of vocational teachers' media-pedagogical competencies and the training of at least 1200 corporate trainers, improving their familiarity with current digital media and fluent application of these media to corporate training.

The creation and use of OER in education have been sponsored by the Ministry of Education and Research since 2006. The Wiki-media Foundation, with financial support from the Ministry, created an OER map in Germany and offered recommendations on four topics: license and legal rights, quality assurance, teacher training, and financial expenditure and business operation.

5.3 Case 3 National Standards to Guide the Sustainable Professional Development of In-Company Trainers: A Case from the Philippines[3]

TVET in the Philippines features a dual training system with learning and training taking place alternately between the vocational intuition and workplace. This system has been instrumental in training highly qualified graduates for the labor market since 1994. In recent years, industrial transformation and changes in labor market demands brought about by the advancement of information technology in Industry 4.0 have presented a range of challenges in upskilling in-company trainers.

The Philippines' Technical Education and Skills Development Authority (TESDA) and the Philippine Chamber of Commerce and Industry (PCCI) developed "Training Regulations" for in-company qualification and trainer competency development based on the 2018 Standard for In-Company Trainer in ASEAN Countries (TESDA, 2021). The "Training Regulations" not only define competency standards for trainers in Philippine enterprises in the Industry 4.0 era, but also serve as a road map for the sustainable development of trainer competencies in enterprises.

5.3.1 The In-Company Trainers Qualification Framework

The "Training Regulations" describes the qualification requirements and competency standards for in-company trainers from four aspects including definition, entry requirements, basic competency requirements, and core competency requirements (Deutsche Gesellschaft für, 2020).

---

[3] Source of this case: Dernbach, A. (2020). Philippine Experience in Dual Training System. In: Panth, B., & Maclean, R. (eds.), Anticipating and Preparing for Emerging Skills and Jobs. Education in the Asia-Pacific Region: Issues, Concerns and Prospects, vol. 55. Springer, Singapore. https://doi.org/10.1007/978-981-15-7018-6_13.

Entry requirements:

- Qualification requirement. If the occupation that students are trained for is regulated by "Training Regulations," the trainer must possess a National Certificate or certification issued either by the company or by the relevant industry association. In addition, a minimum of five years of relevant work experience is required. If the occupation that students are trained for is not regulated by "Training Regulations," the trainer only needs a certification issued either by the company or by the relevant industry association. A minimum of five years of relevant work experience is also required.
- Must have completed grade 10.
- Be capable of reading and writing.
- Be able to perform basic mathematical computation.
- Be able to communicate verbally and non-verbally.

Basic competency requirements. There are 12 competencies required of in-company trainers including:

- leading workplace communication,
- applying math and science principles in technical training,
- applying environmental principles and advocate conservation,
- utilizing IT applications in technical training,
- leading small teams,
- applying work ethics, values, and quality principles,
- working effectively in vocational education and training,
- fostering and promoting a learning culture,
- ensure a healthy and safe learning environment,
- maintaining and enhancing professional practice,
- developing appreciation for cost-benefits of technical training,
- promoting understanding of global labor markets.

Core competency requirements. The core competencies for in-company trainers should be demonstrated in the following four aspects of training:

- Job analysis: analyzing new technologies in the context of digitalization, workplace characteristics, and students' fields of study and needs.
- Preparing for training: analyzing the target trainees of in-company training, determining training contents and learning tasks, selecting appropriate training methods, materials, and facilities (e.g., appropriate digital equipment and tools, digital instructional resources, and teaching methods based on the training content and student characteristics), and simulating a training situation and reflecting on the training process (e.g., designing and using simulation technologies to represent real work environments in the digital world).
- Conducting training: presenting and explaining training contents and learning tasks, using appropriate training methods to monitor and support the trainees' learning process, and formative evaluation on training effectiveness.

- Conducting end-of-training assessments: delivering task-oriented assessments, assessing trainees' competency development, offering and receiving feedback, and continuously improving training.

5.3.2 Emphasizing Digital Competencies in Competency Standards

The competency standards of Philippine in-company trainers emphasize the skills of applying digital technologies in industrial operations and training. On one hand, digital competencies have become a prerequisite for in-company trainers due to changes in corporate work modes, job requirements, and work environments. On the other hand, the development of online teaching, particularly during the pandemic, has increased the demand for in-company trainers with digital technology skills.

5.3.3 Diversified Approaches to In-Company Trainers' Sustainable Professional Development

The "Training Regulations" describe specific competency standards for in-company trainers, as well as methods for obtaining, evaluating, and endorsing these competencies. To promote the sustainable development of their competencies, especially during the pandemic, in-company trainers in the Philippines have adopted many approaches to develop themselves including online learning communities, expert-led seminars, online or offline one-on-one professional support, social media platforms, online courses, OERs, and so on.

5.4 Case 4 A TPACK-Based Integrated Model for Developing TVET Teachers' Professional Competencies—An Example from Shenzhen Polytechnic, China[4]

Shenzhen Polytechnic is a higher vocational institute in Shenzhen Municipality. Founded in 1993, Shenzhen Polytechnic (SZPT) is one of the first colleges in China to independently organize higher vocational and technical education. Based on the dedicated pursuit for integration of industry and education, SZPT has achieved remarkable achievements in providing quality curriculums and has thus become recognized as the "flag-ship" of China's higher vocational education. The institute currently has

---

[4] This case is based on the materials provided by Yang KaiLiang and Yang WengMing, Shenzhen Polytechnic, China.

24,257 full-time students and 2508 faculty members. It offers 85 majors closely in line with the needs of Shenzhen's leading and innovative industries. In view its faculty's needs for a sustained professional development program and guidance, since 2017, Shenzhen Polytechnic has developed an integrated approach to exploring the professional competencies needed by its faculty and strategies to assist faculty to develop these competencies. What is particularly exemplary is the development of an institutional framework specifying the professional competencies required of its teachers. Equally important is their adoption of a training model targeting each of the competences outlined in the proposed framework.

First of all, informed by the TPACK (Technological Pedagogical Content Knowledge) framework (see a discussion of this framework in Sect. 2.2.1), the institute proposed a teachers' professional competency framework (Yang, 2022) that covers both domain knowledge teaching and skill training. There are three constructs in this framework: (1) PCK (Pedagogical Content Knowledge)-based teaching competencies, (2) TPK (Technological Pedagogical Knowledge)-based instructional design competencies, and (3) TCK (Technological Content Knowledge)-based resource integration competencies. PCK-based teaching competencies refer to the pedagogical skills to effectively deliver domain knowledge. TPK-based instructional design competencies involve the capacity to integrate technology into curriculum design for a discipline, a course, or a lesson. TCK-based resource integration competencies encapsulate the capacity to take advantage of technologies to collect, identify, and develop various resources in order to effectively integrate them into curriculum design and delivery. These resources can include, but not limited to, teaching, learning, and training resources, team teaching, and institution-industry collaboration.

Based on this framework, Shenzhen Polytechnic developed the "Integrated Competency Training Model for Vocational Teachers" as shown in Fig. 5.1.

This training model was introduced to help develop vocational teachers' comprehensive capabilities of instructional design, teaching implementation, and resource

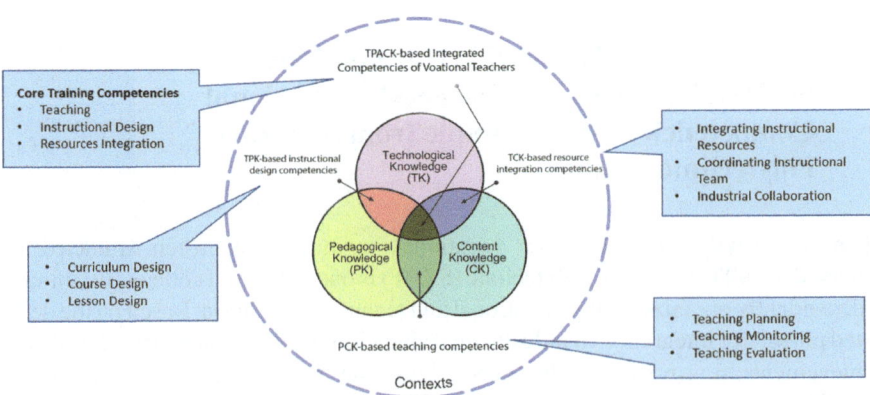

Fig. 5.1 TPACK-based integrated competency training framework for vocational teachers. Adapted from Wang (2010)

integration. It sets specific training objectives and contents for each of the three constructs in the competency framework: PCK-based teaching competencies, TPK-based instructional design competencies, and TCK-based resource integration competencies. This training model has been adopted in the institute's professional development programs since 2018 and it has proven to be highly effective. We will illustrate some of the implementation features of this model using the PCK-based teaching competency training as an example.

Training paradigm. Guided by a task-driven training paradigm, the training provides hands-on learning opportunities for teachers to learn and apply training content in the completion of authentic tasks. These tasks aim to help teachers transfer what they have learned to their teaching practice. The training is offered in modules, and training content is adaptable to suit specific disciplinary requirements. Trainees are also offered opportunities to engage in project-based training in collaboration with industry partners.

Training curriculum design and development. A goal-oriented approach guides the training curriculum design and development. That is, clear learning goals are set at the both the training program level and the instructional activity level to ensure measurable training outcomes.

Approaches to the delivery of training. Guided by theories on individualized learning, authentic learning, and blended learning, a variety of instructional approaches and modalities are adopted to meet the needs of individual teachers. These include project-based learning, task-oriented learning, modular learning, and role-playing. In addition, depending on the training content, a variety of instructional activities are offered during the training. For example, guided reading, online posting, problem-based learning, situated learning, case studies, brainstorming, discussions, concept mapping, and more can be used.

Technology training. Shenzhen Polytechnic adopts the following strategies to promote training and application of technology in teachers' professional development.

(1) Efficient use of smart classrooms for student learning. The institute improves their teaching presentation, students' access to learning resources, and classroom interaction by utilizing smart classrooms that are equipped with technologies such as big data, face recognition, Internet of Things, and artificial intelligence.
(2) Extensive use of XR-based learning spaces. Students can "visualize" and "immerse" themselves in a virtual world by employing technologies such as virtual reality, augmented reality, and mixed reality. Practical and technical skill learning and practice are empowered by the virtual simulation training platform, which allows learners to practice precise operational skills and conduct risky experiments in the virtual environment.
(3) Effective use of the "smart teaching platform." The platform is a big data system that includes management, teaching, evaluation, data feedback, and other

features to improve students' learning outcomes. This platform is valuable in supporting the adoption of the flipped classroom approach in that teachers can actively guide and support students' asynchronous content learning and skill practice before class so that the in-class time can be used more efficiently and effectively. The platform also provides students with a flexible learning space where asynchronous and synchronous activities are available for access at their own pace. Teachers may also use the platform's formative and summative reports to optimize their teaching based on students' feedback.

Training resource development. Shenzhen Polytechnic has taken an integrated approach to the development and design of training resources. This process takes into consideration of the overall planning on the structure, media presentation, and timeline for delivery of the training resources, ensuring that task allocation aligns with the expertise of each team members.

(1) The development of basic instructional resources. Basic instructional resources refer to essential course materials and teaching resources including curriculum standards, textbooks, teaching plans, presentations, micro-videos, exercises, case studies, learning management systems for question banks, and homework.
(2) The development of supplementary instructional resources. These resources refer to teaching resources in addition to basic instructional resources that can supplement teaching and learning, expand learning spaces and venues, and help achieve better learning outcomes. To date, Shenzhen Polytechnic has develop an extensive range of resources including animation, virtual simulation, AR or VR resources, virtual practical training, webinars, repositories of teaching materials and resources, and domain knowledge retrieval systems.

The success of the TPACK-based Integrated Competency Training at Shenzhen Polytechnic has led to a significant improvement in their teachers' instructional design and ICT competencies. The institute has graduated more than 142,000 full-time students up this day, with a 96% or above initial employment rate for their graduates. Their graduates enjoy a greater rate of employment in the world's top 500 companies, a higher rate of innovation and entrepreneurship, and a higher starting salary compared with their peers in the country.

5.5 Case 5 A Standard-Based Tiered Training System in Support of Teachers' ICT Competency Development: A Case from Chengdu Vocational and Technical College, China[5]

Chengdu Vocational and Technical College (CVTC) was founded in 2003. It consists of seven disciplinary groups such as software technology, smart tourism, intelligent construction, and smart health care, offering 38 programs with a strong link to local industries. CVTC currently has about 11,000 students, 597 full-time teachers, and 202 adjunct teachers. In order to enhance faculty's digital competencies and promote the effective use of technology in teaching, CVTC developed their "Faculty ICT Competency Standards," based on which to provide tiered training and resources for faculty of different career phrases.

CVTC published its provisional version of "Faculty ICT Competency Standards" in 2021. The standards outline the specific requirements for faculty's information literacy competence and practical skills in five areas: responsibility and awareness, curriculum and instruction, tools and their application, evaluation and improvement, and research and innovation. The standards also serve as a guide for designing training programs and developing online training courses and e-textbooks.

In their efforts to normalize faculty's ICT competence development, CVTC has created a four-tier training system based on faculty's years of work and teaching experience. The system targets at four groups of faculty: new faculty, faculty with three years of employment at the institute, faculty with teaching experience for more than five years, and senior faculty. To cater for the specific needs of each group, three levels of training are designed: the beginning, medium and advanced levels, which correspond to the three levels of competency requirements specified in the "Faculty ICT Competency Standards."

In addition, CVTC hosts training programs on a variety of topics, including training teachers for participating in the institutional, provincial/municipal and national levels of competitions for best ICT-supported teaching practices (see Case 1 for details of these competitions), the development and application of electronic textbooks, effective resources for mobile devices, PowerPoint design and application, and the design of micro-lessons, etc. Faculty from each college and department take turns participating in online and face-to-face training. Their annual training includes teaching and ICT competence training for faculty and technicians (over 400 participants per year), information technology training for students (including network security, with overall 5000 participants per year), and training for enterprise partners (with over 500 participants per year).

CVTC takes advantage of many learning platforms to provide training opportunities, including UMOOC, XuetangX, Mosoink, and Qinghua Online. Aside from

---

[5] This case is based on the materials provided by Huang Lu, Chengdu Vocational and Technical College, China.

that, they also invite external experts to offer a series of lectures covering the five areas recommended by the "Faculty ICT Competency Standards" (see above).

Those training opportunities guide faculty in applying ICT theories to their teaching, supporting educational reform, effectively integrating technology tools into their teaching, and enhancing instructional quality.

CVTC also encourages faculty to develop their professional competencies via various other instructional resources and opportunities. For example, faculty are encouraged to participate in national teaching competitions to innovate their pedagogy and learn from their colleagues. They are also encouraged to develop and use various virtual simulation resources in their teaching. Following their initiatives on blended learning reform, CVTC has engendered asynchronous and synchronous opportunities for the competency training and for faculty teaching on several online platforms. Besides, CVTC faculty are also supported to develop their cloud-based textbooks, demonstrating a high level of ICT proficiency. To recognize their faculty's professional development efforts, CVTC has developed their own system of certifying faculty's ICT competencies based on their levels and duration of training.

Intensive online training is another feature of CVTC's professional development for their teachers. For example, between October and November 2021, the institute offered 10 intensive online training sessions, each lasting five days. With an emphasis on blended learning, these courses were designed for all academic teachers with the aim to strengthen their ICT competencies. The training was delivered via their online learning platform covering topics on blended learning design, micro video and online resource development, effective use of concept mapping tools, and PowerPoint design and application.

CVTC's standard-based, customized training system has greatly improved their faculty's ICT competence and their instructional design skills. Their teachers won several awards in the National Competition for Best ICT Supported Teaching Practices in 2020–2021, while their students have received numerous prizes in the Vocational Skill Competitions and Innovative Entrepreneurship Competitions. CVTC's innovative training programs have been recognized nationally for their efforts in teachers' professional development.

5.6 Case 6 A Top-Down Model of Developing TVET Teachers' Digital Teaching Competencies: Strategies Adopted by Shouguang Vocational School, China[6]

Shouguan Vocational School is a state-run school located in Weifang, Shangdong Province, with 490 teaching staff and over 7000 students. It offers practical and industry-relevant courses and subjects across a range of skills relating to computer

---

[6] This case is based on the materials provided by Wang JiaYang, Shouguang Vocational School, China.

science, agriculture, information technology, pre-school education, oceanology, and many other training programs.

As a comparatively new school, it has faced a number of challenges in teachers' professional development. Among them, lack of motivation, clear orientation, and sustained efforts have been identified by the school as the key areas for improvement. Since 2016, the school has adopted a top-down approach to develop a sustainable model to help teachers in their professional development.

Developing digital teaching competence for all teachers was one of the priorities in the school's Strategic Plan 2016–2020. The school started to implement blended learning in 2016 under the guidance and support of the Institute of Education, Tsinghua University and UMOOC company. Since then, the school has actively participated in a range of projects relating to blended learning and online course and resource development at both the provincial and national level such as the Blended Learning Development Strategy project, Digital Campus Building project, and Quality Open Online Course project. These projects informed the school's strategic decision to include the development of teachers' digital teaching competencies into its blended learning initiative, making it parallel with the development of digitalization of learning content and innovation in teaching and learning evaluation.

The school has developed a model consisting of four key strategies and stages (Fig. 5.2). As shown in Fig. 5.2, the four strategies are institution-wide training, teaching competitions, ongoing PD activities, and data-driven evaluation. This model also recognizes the progressive and transformative nature of teachers' digital teaching competency growth from awareness (becoming conscious of the need for ICT enhanced learning), exploration (beginning to understand the pedagogical potential of ICT), adoption (applying ICT in teaching), and innovation (creative use of ICT).

In view of the limitations in the previous professional development program, such as limited coverage, outdated contents, lack of effective application of training outcomes to practice, the school management decided to engage an external team of trainers to develop a series of school-wide initiatives to prepare staff in terms of blended learning pedagogy in 2017. The team of trainers consisted of researchers and practitioners in blended learning pedagogy as well as IT support personnel. The first initiative started in March 2017, when a blended learning workshop was delivered by external blended learning researchers and practitioners. In April 2017, the school called for expression of interest from academic staff to participate in blended learning pedagogy training and selected 20 as seed teachers. These teachers watched 18 online modules on blended learning course design and designed and delivered their own blended learning courses with the online support of the training team. In May 2017, the training team came to the school to discuss, face to face, with each of the 20 teachers on specific issues encountered in their blended teaching. These teachers attended an advanced workshop at Tsinghua University in July 2017 to further develop their digital teaching competency and reflect on their experiences and learning.

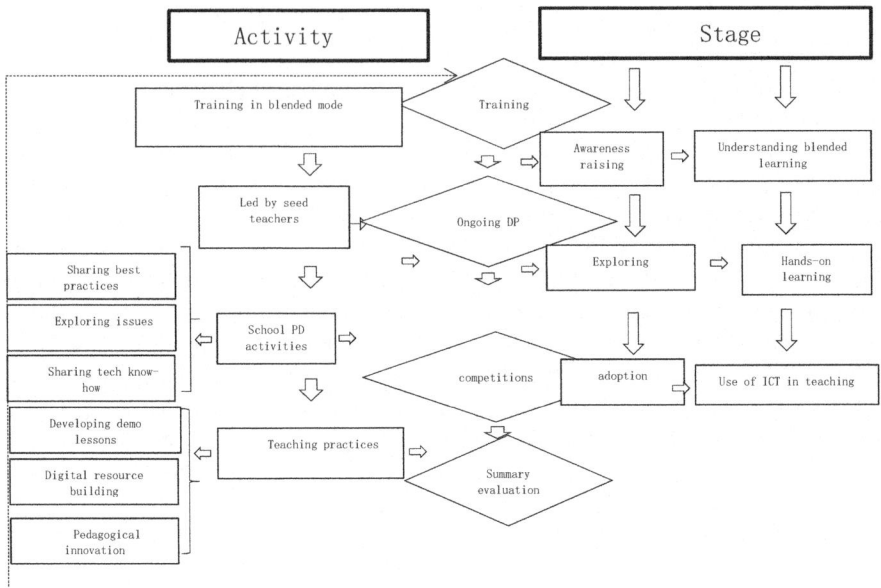

Fig. 5.2 A top-down model of developing TVET teachers' digital teaching competencies

Since July 2017, these seed teachers have shared their experiences and insights through a range of school-wide activities such as demo classes, seminars and workshops showcasing exemplary teaching practices, discussing challenges in ICT adoption, and sharing new insights into blended learning pedagogy and strategies. These activities have helped new blended learning adopters and future adopters in the school to better understand the potential and importance of blended learning.

At the same time, all the training materials have been uploaded to the school's Learning Management System (LMS). To date, there are over 200 training repositories available online covering theories and pedagogy relating to blended and online learning, demo classes, technical support resources, and recordings of seminars by experts. These resources can be used for school-wide ongoing training activities as well as for individual teachers' self-development in digital teaching competency.

In order to further promote teachers' blended and online teaching competencies, the school systematically organizes and supports teachers to participate in various teaching competitions. These competitions range from national, provincial, municipal, and school-based ones. The school also encourages its teachers to form a community of practice where seed teachers guide and support other teachers from various fields of study in preparation for these competitions. This practice has become an ongoing part of the school's professional development programs.

To facilitate the blended learning implementation, the school has made efforts to assist teachers to more effectively manage online resources, online tests, online forums, and survey instruments.

Digital teaching competence becomes a key performance indicator (KPI) for academic staff and for the performance review of all departments in the school. Each semester, the school's overall performance data in blended and online teaching are published, and the completion rate of the integration of ICT into curricula is assessed and published monthly. These results are used to assess staff performance monthly and annually.

In the past five years, blended learning approaches and strategies have been integrated into the curricula of every disciplinary area. Blended learning has now become an integral part of the school's teaching. ICT has been embedded in curricula in a manner consistent with course requirements and learning outcomes.

5.7 Case 7 An Integrated and Coordinated Approach to Developing Teachers' Professional competencies—A Case from Baden-Wuerttemberg Cooperative State University in Germany[7]

As a direct successor to Baden-Württemberg vocational college, Baden-Wuerttemberg Cooperative State University (BHBW) is a dual-education institution in Germany, offering degrees in cooperation with industry and non-profit institutions. The university offers a broad range of undergraduate study programs in the field of business, engineering, and social work and also offers postgraduate degree programs with integrated on-the-job training. All degree programs are both nationally and internationally accredited. BHBW has around 33,500 enrolled students, over 9000 partner companies, and more than 200,000 graduates.

In response to the changes in the competency requirements of the labor market in the digital age, DHBW has adopted a range of digital media tools in teaching and learning to improve learning outcomes. Such an extensive use of ICT requires teachers not only to acquire sufficient digital literacy, but also to develop technology-enhanced pedagogy to improve their teaching quality. To help teachers develop these competencies, DHBW has implemented a variety of strategies including clarifying goals for teachers' competency development, establishing support structures, developing additional resources, and developing and improving assessment mechanisms for evaluating teachers' competency development.

---

[7] Source of this case: DHBW. Wir über uns. [2019-06-10] [2022-03-15]. https://www.dhbw.de/die-dhbw/wirueber-uns.

5.7.1 Clarifying Goals for Faculty Teaching Competency Development

In collaboration with their corporate partners, DHBW has offered its students a dual-study mode allowing learning and skill training to alternate between the classroom and workplace. This mode enables students to gain both theoretical knowledge and practical skills during their study in DHBW. DHBW has developed a blended learning approach to support the dual-study mode through various digital media technology tools. Digital technologies are not only used in the classroom, but also in teaching and learning management such as submitting research papers, assigning advisers, maintaining teaching logs, and administering digitalized tests. Thus, DHBW clarifies and emphasizes the following goals in promoting teachers' teaching competencies: (a) continuing to raise teachers' awareness of the potential of ICT and technological equipment, (b) integrating ICT and technological equipment in view of catering for the specific disciplinary needs and learners' needs for diversified and personalized learning, and (c) innovating pedagogy and teaching modes.

5.7.2 Creating Support Structures to Develop Faculty Teaching Competencies

DHBW established the Center for Teaching and Lifelong Learning to support the development of their teachers' teaching competencies. Its major areas of services include teaching and learning, faculty development, and assessment of qualifications. In terms of faculty development, the Center has:

- supported teachers' teaching competency development through offering training programs and professional development activities (e.g., how to teach online, how to manage student inquiries). These training programs are offered on their online continuing education platform where teachers can also post new ideas and share their teaching experiences in the online forum called "Online Teaching Café." The Center also issues certificates of online professional development to teachers who have completed those trainings.
- produced a series of publications to encourage the exchange of innovative teaching ideas and experiences. Topics range from the introduction of various teaching principles and practices, approaches to online teaching and learning, and how to integrate theory into practice.
- conducted online and in-person teaching seminars and programs to develop their teachers' teaching competencies and optimize student learning outcomes.

5.7.3 Developing Resources for Enhancing Teaching Competencies

DHBW has developed various resources to support the development of their teachers' ICT competencies. The DHBW Teaching Handbook and its supplementary resource, Practical Templates for the Teaching Handbook are two good examples.

The DHBW Teaching Handbook provides guidance for teachers in areas such as media-enhanced instructional design and delivery, exams, and curriculum planning.

The Practical Templates for the Teaching Handbook has also proved useful for teachers to track students' learning process, adopt appropriate teaching methods, select appropriate digital media tools, design and deliver online teaching, and plan the overall curriculum of a course.

5.7.4 Developing and Improving Assessment Mechanisms for Evaluating Teachers' Competency Development

In 2018, DHBW published its updated edition of "Quality Management Handbook," which provides guidance for developing teachers' teaching competencies as well as a set of mechanisms for assessing teachers' competency development. Key indicators for measuring teachers' professional development were introduced in these mechanisms. They include providing integrated internal and external evaluation, updating teacher qualification criteria and responsibilities, providing standards for outstanding teaching practice, offering teaching evaluations (of application of digital media technologies, students' learning outcomes, and various assessments used in teaching), and covering an instructional development quality report.

5.7.5 Characteristics of DHBW's Systematic Approach

(1) **Identifying teaching competency constructs and recognizing the importance of sustained teachers' professional development**. One of the primary goals of DHBW is to ensure that their students graduate with the skills needed in the current labor market and are competent in their occupations. This goal led to the creation of the "Quality Assurance Handbook," which considers the entire quality assurance of the institution. The handbook clearly articulates the competencies required of their teachers of all levels, as well as standards for the use of digital media tools, course evaluation, evaluation of assessment methods, teaching evaluation report, and so on.

(2) **Promoting student-centered instructional design and delivery, and evaluation of teaching and learning**. The emphasis of current teaching in DHBW has shifted from knowledge imparting by the teacher to active learning by the

student, resulting in a transition from teaching-cantered to learning-cantered pedagogy. Their goal of instruction is to assist students in acquiring knowledge and developing their vocational skills. Thus, DHBW recognizes the importance for their teachers to know what knowledge and skills future graduates need in the digital age. Accordingly, their teachers' professional development has been focusing on the innovative use of digital technologies in teaching and supporting students in acquiring those skills. To better meet students' needs, teachers in DHBW are supported in the institute's professional development programs in developing proficiency in utilizing various technologies to innovate curriculum and instructional design, delivery approaches, online assessments, and teaching evaluation.

(3) **Linking theory to practice in teachers' professional development**. The DHBW Teaching Handbook introduces guidelines for instructional design and implementation of ICT-supported teaching and learning and provides cases and examples of how to apply them in practice. This has been achieved through theoretical expositions followed by practical procedures and examples. In addition, the Practical Templates for the Teaching Handbook also includes templates and scaffoldings for faculty to use in designing, implementing, and reflecting on their teaching practices. For example, faculty can use the templates to categorize and present teaching contents for face-to-face and online teaching in an integrated manner to optimize content delivery. Faculty can also use the self-evaluation form on the templates to assess their level of preparation with reference to the selection of teaching resources, the use of digital media and tools and the adoption of instructional methods.

5.8 Case 8 College-Enterprise Cooperative Training Based on TVET Teaching Competency Standards: A Case from China[8]

5.8.1 Background

U-MOOC Online Education Technology (Beijing) Co., Ltd. was established at the end of 2014. It is a national high-tech company that specializes in the research, design, development, application, and evaluation of online learning platform learning management system. The system provides an overall e-Learning solution for 500 universities and vocational colleges with an emphasis on the continuous improvement of their teachers' digital teaching capabilities.

---

[8] The draft material was prepared by Zhou Qian, Qinghua University.

5.8.2 Development of the College-Enterprise Cooperation

Guided by TVET teaching competency standards, the college-enterprise cooperation is distinctive and innovative in its training philosophies, goals, and methods. Its philosophy involves promoting vocational teachers' digital teaching competency as well as the integration of technology for teaching such as the IT application theories in blended learning. The training design team analyzes the digital teaching competency of their teachers based on TVET Teaching Competency Standards and urgent needs of the target audience.

The goal of the training is to enhance the teaching competency of individual teachers and promote the team building of the teachers. According to China's State Council's National Vocational Education Reform program (hereafter referred to as "20 Articles of TVET"), we should adapt to the demands of "Internet + vocational education" and use current information technology to enhance the instructional performance (China's State Council, 2019). Workshop-based vocational teacher training aims to enhance vocational teacher's competencies of course development, course delivery, professional knowledge, industrial capability, information literacy, and research and development. The training design team analyzes the teaching competencies of vocational teachers based on the TVET Teaching Competency Standards, and then designs tailored training programs based on the findings. Vocational colleges can promote their teachers' communication and develop an environment of teaching discovery in the information age by holding experience-sharing sessions, forums, and workshops. Vocational colleges can encourage their teachers to apply their comprehensive teaching ability in their classrooms by incorporating teaching delivery, student satisfaction, and academic achievement into teacher performance appraisal indicators, resulting in improved vocational teachers' comprehensive teaching competencies through training and teaching practice.

The six dimensions and four phases have been proposed as the framework of TVET teachers' competency in the digital age that can be applied to the establishment of training goals (see Chap. 3).

The training has been conducted using the "standard-led, situation-based, and personalized design" teacher development approach to promote the development of teachers' teaching competency in the information age. Figure 5.3 shows how phases flow.

Based on dimensions and standards of the teaching competency of vocational teachers, an index system and an assessment scale were used as a benchmark and tools for diagnosing and evaluating vocational colleges and their teachers' teaching competency of using Information and Communication Technology (ICT).

Teachers were classified into different phases of development based on their evaluation results. Follow-up plans were also created to improve their teaching skills based on their current teaching situations. The systematic development of vocational teachers' teaching competency has aided in the development and innovation of the academic programs, as well as providing assurance for effective hybrid teaching reform and development. The standardization of teaching competency standards for

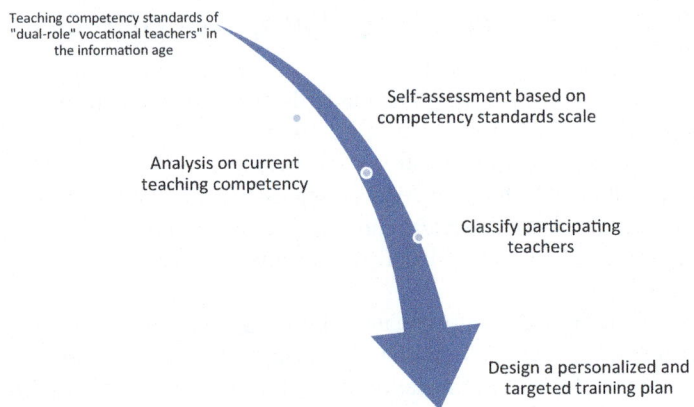

Fig. 5.3 "Standard-led, situation-based, and personalized design" teacher development approach

vocational teachers is one of the breakthroughs in leading the development of vocational education, improving the vocational education system, and establishing and improving school curricula, teaching staff, teaching materials, and application of ICT in teaching. The personalized design of training programs and the systematic planning of training content are two examples of training innovations.

U-MOOC presented a long-term, systematic, personalized, and actionable teacher development program with personalized design at its center. With response to participating teachers' needs, the system was designed to fulfill the teachers' training demands. U-MOOC facilitated a network among vocational institutions by forming a service team that includes training supervisors, specialists, corporate representatives, and more. They also collaborate to solve problems, build a stable long-term partnership, and train teachers towards teaching experts.

U-MOOC classified teachers' development into four phases based on vocational teachers' teaching competency standard framework: beginners to advanced beginners, advanced beginners to competent teachers, competent to resourceful teachers, and resourceful teachers to teaching experts, with a total of 56 specified indicators. The four phases of development correspond to four levels of learning evaluation in Kirkpatrick Model and the COMET Competence Model. The "beginners to advanced beginners" phase corresponds to the layers of teachers' reaction and learning. The "advanced beginners to competent teachers" phase corresponds to the behavioural change layer. The "competent to resourceful teachers" and "resourceful teachers to teaching experts" phases correspond to the results layer.

(1) **Beginners to advanced beginners**

The beginners to advanced beginners' phase focuses on gaining a basic understanding of course development, course delivery, professional knowledge, information literacy, and research and development. In this phase, through hands-on approaches, teachers will adjust their teaching philosophy and understand the characteristics of vocational educational curriculum and teaching in the information age.

In this phase, four modules are available for teacher development offered through cooperation between on-campus teacher development offices and external educational service units. Modules in this phase are mainly delivered in the form of expert lectures, case sharing, exercises, and expert reviews. The specific training formats and modules are shown in Table 5.1. Each vocational school will select trainings from the list suitable for their teachers based on the analysis of their current teaching competency.

(2) **Advanced beginners to competent teachers**

The phase of advanced beginners to competent teachers mostly involves teaching preparation and implementation. Training in this phase is customarily provided through online Q & A and engagement in experiential learning. With no predefined training material, training content is the same as it is in the beginners to advanced beginner phase. Training is mostly conducted through individualized one-on-one online consultations or small-group meetings based on participants' questions.

(3) **Competent to resourceful teachers**

Transiting from competent to resourceful teachers, teachers should have a greater grasp of course development, course delivery, information literacy, and research and development. This is a result of as having sufficient vocational educational reform experience from prior rounds of training, As a result, some exemplary instructors with prior experience in teaching reform may have higher expectations for their self-value to be realized.

Various vocational teaching competency and lecture contests are held regularly at the college, municipal, provincial, and national levels. Besides, there are also opportunities for vocational teachers to apply research and instructional development funding. Teachers in this transition need to consolidate their teaching reform experiences, data, and reflections into "teaching achievements" which is a unique undertaking that demands them to combine theory and practice. Teachers are now more anxious to master vocational education curriculum and instructional theories, as well as theories on ICT integration and other foundational educational pedagogyy. In many cases, due to their heavy teaching loads and administrative responsibilities, teachers can only refer to teaching pedagogy resources when preparing for "special events" such as "teaching skill competition," "young teachers teaching competition," "lecture competition," and "teaching achievements award."

As a result, training in this phase mainly focused on theories that are closely related to instructional practices such as vocational education curriculum and teaching theories, theories on ICT integration, and systematic research and development theories. This training phase is critical for developing teachers' teaching competencies as they pilot and adjust to best new teaching practices based on learning theories.

This phase of training is designed to help teachers break out of their comfort zones by helping them to systematically understand learning theories, practice applying those theories in their teaching, reflect on and create new best practices as they implement ICT in the classroom, and ultimately, become teaching experts in their fields. The modules in this phase are mainly delivered through expert lectures, case

Table 5.1 Teacher development module for beginners to advanced beginners

Modules	Topics	Formats	Length (h)
1. Course development	Vocational educational job analysis	Seminar	1.5
	Typical task analysis in vocational education	Seminar	1.5
	Vocational education curriculum system	Seminar	1.5
	Vocational educational curriculum development	Seminar	1.5
	Occupational warehouse and its application in education	Seminar	1.5
	Design project-based hybrid curriculum	Workshop	2
	Develop project-based hybrid curriculum	Workshop	2
2. Course delivery	Design and optimize instructional design worksheet	Workshop	2
	Hybrid course design practice	Workshop	2
	Course design worksheet discussions and case sharing	Workshop	2
	Instructional evaluation design (course evaluation design, instructional outcome evaluation design)	Workshop	1.5
	The industry-education collaboration in vocational education	Experience sharing	1.5
	Research and practice on multi-mode hybrid teaching in vocational colleges	Seminar	1.5
	Research and practice in hybrid teaching implementation in vocational colleges	Seminar	1.5
	Application of participation methods in teaching	Workshop	1.5
	Hybrid teaching mode and cases	Experience sharing	1.5
	The organization and implementation of hybrid teaching	Workshop	1.5
	Experience a better classroom-hybrid teaching exploration and practice	Experience sharing	1.5
	Research and practice on hybrid teaching reform	Seminar	1.5
	Systematic research and practice on hybrid teaching in vocational colleges	Seminar	1.5
	Research and development of digital learning environment	Seminar	1.5
	Design and practice of PBL (project-based learning)	Workshop	1.5

(continued)

Table 5.1 (continued)

Modules	Topics	Formats	Length (h)
	Make your classroom full of passion, wisdom, and joy-discussions on teaching methods and teaching art	Experience sharing	1.5
	Formative assessment supported by online learning platforms	Workshop	1.5
3. Information literacy	Excellent case sharing	Experience sharing	1.5
	Guide on ICT in teaching	Seminar	1.5
	The comparative advantage of vocational education in internet + era	Seminar	1.5
	Design and production of micro videos using video recording software	Workshop	2
	Using mind mapping software	Workshop	2
	PPT optimization skills	Workshop	2
	Using live steaming tools	Workshop	2
	Using online integrated education platform	Workshop	2
	Using online evaluation tools	Workshop	2
	Application of mobile learning	Workshop	2
	Production of instructional resources	Workshop	2
	Access and use of open educational resources	Workshop	1.5
	Ethics of application of information technology in teaching	Seminar	1.5
	Hybrid teaching: from instrumental rational to value rational	Seminar	1.5
4. Research and development	Design LMS-based research	Workshop	1.5
	Questionnaire design and application	Workshop	1.5
	Quantitative data in teaching research	Workshop	1.5
	Qualitative data in teaching research	Workshop	1.5
	Foundational methods of teaching research	Workshop	1.5
	Hybrid teaching research methods	Workshop	1.5
	Teaching and research thesis writing	Workshop	1.5
	Guides on paper publication	Workshop	1.5
	Practical tools for online teaching and research	Workshop	1.5
	Research on systematic application of ICT in teaching	Seminar	1.5
	Exploration of hybrid teaching competency development	Seminar	1.5

(continued)

Table 5.1 (continued)

Modules	Topics	Formats	Length (h)
	New challenges in new modes of vocational education	Seminar	1.5
	Research on the teaching competency standards of "dual-role" vocational teachers in the information age	Seminar	1.5
	20 Articles of TVET for the development of vocational colleges	Seminar	1.5
	Professional ethics education	Seminar	1.5

sharing, workshops, and more. The specific training formats and modules are shown in Tables 5.2.

In this phase, faculty training can be structured in a variety of ways, including mixing instructors' personal study with external training. Teachers can self-learn using a variety of online training tools. External training plans with focused theories are created based on instructors' present teaching skills.

(4) **Resourceful teachers to expert teachers**

The key duties in the previous three phases have been fulfilled by teachers in the phase of resourceful teachers to expert teachers. Based on their experience in vocational educational curriculum and teaching reform, research achievements, and peer recognition, they are exceptional in their job and becoming experts in their disciplines. Teachers in this phase are not confined to conducting small-scale individual study; instead, through continuous learning and communication they can gain more knowledge and develop their own vocational educational instructional theory system that can be utilized in various contexts. Vocational colleges for those experts should provide them with a platform where they may influence others and contribute to the development of other teachers.

5.8.3 Results

A review of current vocational teachers' teaching competencies in the information age revealed some problems and issues in the past teacher development. Issues regarding training delivery include: (1) no tailored training addressing participants' needs, (2) prioritizing training length above quality, (3) no follow-up on training content, (4) training content cannot be applied to teaching practice, (5) too much content in a short period of time, (6) theory is disconnected from practice and cannot be easily applied, (7) training content is not thorough enough, (8) irresponsible training experts with ill-prepared materials, (9) no ongoing training or communication with training experts, (10) a lack of focus in training, (11) no training objectives,

Table 5.2 Teacher development module for competent to resourceful teachers

Module	Topic	Formats	Length (h)
1. Course development	Theories on vocational education job analysis	Seminar	1.5
	Vocational education curriculum development theories (DACUM curriculum development methods)	Seminar	1.5
	Research on qualification of curriculum development	Seminar	1.5
	Theories on typical job analysis	Seminar	1.5
	Theories on developing vocational educational curriculum system	Seminar	1.5
	Theories on developing project-based vocational educational curriculum	Seminar	1.5
2. Course delivery	Hybrid teaching philosophies, goals, and principles	Seminar	1.5
	Theories on bloom's taxonomy of learning objectives	Seminar	1.5
	Scaffolding in teaching	Seminar	1.5
	Philosophies and development of open educational resources	Seminar	1.5
	Theories on instructional methods	Seminar	1.5
	Action-oriented teaching theories	Seminar	1.5
	Theories on teaching evaluation	Seminar	1.5
	Theories on course evaluation	Seminar	1.5
3. Information literacy	Application of ICT in solving teaching problems	Seminar	1.5
	Theories on application of ICT in teaching	Seminar	1.5
	Hybrid teaching theories	Seminar	1.5
	Online education theories	Seminar	1.5
	Learning theories on media application	Seminar	1.5
4. Research and development	Funding topic selection and application	Workshop	2
	Application of teaching research award	Workshop	2
	Integration of teacher development theories and experience on self-development	Experience sharing	2
	Introduction of award-winning courses	Experience sharing	2
	Experience sharing of teaching competency competition of vocational teachers	Experience sharing	2
	Professional ethics education based on theories and practices	Experience sharing	2

(12) delivering teaching innovation with outdated teaching methods, and (13) no interaction.

Participants' identified several training demands identified in the survey. First, they desired course development training on hybrid course design and textbook development (such as loose-leaf textbooks). Training on information literacy in online course development, workplace practices, mind mapping, software application, ICT application, and design of educational resources such as animation and min-games, PPT design, and web development would be helpful. Course delivery training such as design of teaching evaluation, hybrid teaching, teaching methods and strategies, innovative instructional activities, and using instructional practice guidance rather than lecturing were some areas identified in the survey as valuable professional development areas. Finally, the participants indicated that training on industrial practice skills and research and development (e.g., training on research tools and interpretation of vocational education policy) were preferred.

Training effectiveness is mainly measured by post-tests and satisfaction surveys. There are 5 multiple-choice questions and 9 short-answer questions on the post-test. The questions in the post-test are different, yet comparable from the ones in pre-test. Participants are tested on the four training themes with a total of 100 points. The post-test is graded with graders of the pre-test following a criterion. Test results indicated that participating teachers performed best in the information literacy section and may need to work on their course design skills.

A satisfaction survey using a 5-point Likert Scale and open-ended questions was used to find out participating teachers' general perceptions of the training, satisfaction towards various training courses, as well as suggestions. A total of 34 teachers completed the survey with a 100% completion rate and a Cronbach coefficient of 0.791. Overall satisfaction and degree of satisfaction in all areas are high and more than 50% of respondents were highly satisfied in most questions.

5.8.4 Reflections

Cooperation between vocational colleges and enterprises can serve to provide a formation of a professional training team to assist the development of teachers' competencies and practices. The demands of vocational teacher training can be met by improving vocational teachers' ICT teaching competency.

Course development, course delivery, information literacy, and research and development are the only four primary areas covered in the present training, and training on disciplinary knowledge and industry competencies is currently unavailable. Furthermore, current training emphasizes skills in using ICT in the classroom, and future training should include content that can be thoroughly interwoven with specific academic programs. It will eventually serve as a reference tool for evaluating vocational teachers' teaching competencies, as well as examples for providing self-study and professional development programs.

References

ASEAN. (2018). *Standard for in-company trainers in ASEAN countries*. [2022-03-21]. https://www.bibb.de/dokumente/pdf/ab1.2_standard_in-companytrainers_ASEAN_regions.pdf

Breiter, A., Howe, F., & Hartel, M. (2017). *Media-pedagogical competence of company-based training staff*. https://www.bibb.de/en/61493.php

Bundesministerium für Bildung und Forschung. *Die Neue Hightech-Strategie Innovationen für Deutschland*. (2014). https://www.bmbf.de/bmbf/shareddocs/downloads/upload_filestore/pub_hts/hts_broschure_web.pdf?__blob=publicationFile&v=1

China's State Council. (2019). *Notice of the state council's issuance of the national vocational education reform program*. [2019-02-13] [2020-09-23]. http://www.gov.cn/zhengce/content/2019-02/13/content_5365341.htm

Deutsche Gesellschaft für Internationale Zusammenarbeit (GIZ) GmbH. (2020). *The technical education and skills development authority, & the Philippine chamber of commerce and industry. Implementing the standard for in-company trainers in ASEAN countries—Country case studies: Philippines*. [2022-03-21]. https://www.plattform-i40.de/IP/Navigation/EN/Home/home.html

Federal Ministry for Economic Affairs and Climate Action. What is the plattform industrie 4.0? https://www.plattformi40.de/IP/Navigation/EN/Home/home.html

TESDA (2021). The TVET trainer in the future of work and learning. Labor Market Intelligence Report. Technical Education and Skills Development Authority (TESDA), Issue no. 2, Series of 2021.. [2022-03-21]. https://tesda.gov.ph/Uploads/File/LMIR/2021/LMIR%20on%20Skills%20of%20TVET%20Trainers.pdf

Tulodziecki, G., Herzig, B., & Grafe, S. (2019). Medienbildung in Schule und Unterricht. Julius Klinkhardt, Bad Heilbrunn

Wang, J. (2010). *Structures of nonlinear learning spaces*.

Yang, K. (2022). *TPACK-based integrated competency training framework for vocational teachers*. Training report from Shenzhen Polytechnic

Open Access This chapter is licensed under the terms of the Creative Commons Attribution-NonCommercial-NoDerivatives 4.0 International License (http://creativecommons.org/licenses/by-nc-nd/4.0/), which permits any noncommercial use, sharing, distribution and reproduction in any medium or format, as long as you give appropriate credit to the original author(s) and the source, provide a link to the Creative Commons license and indicate if you modified the licensed material. You do not have permission under this license to share adapted material derived from this chapter or parts of it.

The images or other third party material in this chapter are included in the chapter's Creative Commons license, unless indicated otherwise in a credit line to the material. If material is not included in the chapter's Creative Commons license and your intended use is not permitted by statutory regulation or exceeds the permitted use, you will need to obtain permission directly from the copyright holder.

Glossary of Terms

Assessment instrument An assessment instrument is the documented activities developed to support assessment methods and used to collect the evidence of student learning outcomes. An assessment instrument could include: oral and written questions, observation/demonstration checklists, projects, case studies, scenarios or workplace portfolios.

Australian Government Australian Skills Quality Authority. *What is the difference between an assessment tool and an assessment instrument?* https://www.asqa.gov.au/faqs/what-difference-between-assessment-tool-and-assessment-instrument-clause-18

Competency Competence refers to the combination of one's knowledge, skills and personal attributes such as attitudes, disposition, beliefs and values, that makes one professionally competent (Koster & Dengerink, 2008) (see Sect. 2.1.2).

Koster, B., & Dengerink, J. J. (2008). Professional standards for teacher educators: how to deal with complexity, ownership and function. Experiences from the Netherlands. *European Journal of Teacher Education, 31*(2), 135–149.

Curriculum Curriculum, in the briefest meaning of the term, is a course of studies, or what is to be taught.

Richey, R. C. (2013). *Encyclopedia of terminology for educational communications and technology* (pp. 74). Springer.

Digital transformation of education A series of deep and coordinated cultural, workforce, and technology shifts that enable new educational and operating models and transform an institution's operations, strategic directions, and value proposition.

Christopher, D. B., & Mccormack, M. *Driving digital transformation in higher education [EB/OL]*. (2020-06-15) [2022-1-1]. https://library.educause.edu/resources/2020/6/driving-digital-transformation-in-higher-education

DIY learning DIY learning is self-organized learning based on the work scene. DIY learning might potentially facilitate teachers' ICT-enabled, lifelong, personalized, adaptive and just-in-time learning.

UNESCO. (1972). *Learn to be—The world of education today and tomorrow.* UNESCO. Paris 1972.

Indicator It is a marker of accomplishment/progress. It is a specific, observable, and measurable accomplishment or change that shows the progress made toward achieving a specific output or outcome in a logic model or work plan.

Developing Evaluation Indicators. https://www.cdc.gov/std/Program/pupestd/Developing%20Evaluation%20Indicators.pdf

Micro-credentials Micro-credentials recognize a specific set of learning outcomes in a narrow field of learning and achieved over a short period of time. Micro-credentials are offered by commercial entities, private providers, professional bodies, education and training providers, community organizations and other types of organizations. While many micro-credentials represent the outcomes of more traditional learning experiences, others verify demonstration of achievements acquired elsewhere, such as in the workplace, through volunteering, or through personal interest learning. Micro-credentials are often promoted as an efficient way to upskill workers across the lifespan (see Sect. 2.2.4).

UNESCO. (2021, September). *A conversation starter: Towards a common definition of micro-credentials.* https://vital.voced.edu.au/vital/access/services/Download/ngv:91634/SOURCE201

Open educational resources (OER) Open educational resources (OER) are learning, teaching and research materials in any format and medium that reside in the public domain or are under copyright that have been released under an open license, that permit no-cost access, re-use, re-purpose, adaptation and redistribution by others.

UNESCO. (2019, November 25). *Recommendation concerning open educational resources.* Retrieved from http://portal.unesco.org/en/ev.php-URL_ID=49556&URL_DO=DO_TOPIC&URL_SECTION=201.html

Standard Standards are considered as norms, requirements and quality measuring tools. They aim to clarify the expected development goals of specific things in the field of education, and reflect the characteristics of being widely known, leading to action and avoiding irrational coercion.

Bergmann, M. (2011). Standards for quality in education. Experiences from different countries and lessons learnt [R]. Deutsche Gesellschaft für Internationale Zusammenarbeit (GIZ) GmbH.

Teacher learning communities Teacher learning communities are social groupings of new and experienced educators who come together over time for the purpose of gaining new information, reconsidering previous knowledge and beliefs, and building on their own and others' ideas and experiences in order to work on a specific agenda intended to improve practice and enhance students' learning in K–12 schools and other educational settings (see Sect. 2.3.5).

Teacher Learning Communities. (n.d.). Retrieved May 13, 2022, from https://education.stateuniversity.com/pages/2483/Teacher-Learning-Communities.html

Teacher training Teacher training is generally used to describe the courses and qualifications that teachers undertake and receive in their careers, or one-off courses that are largely designed with a short-term or immediate purpose in mind.

Breen, P. (2014). *An intramuscular approach to teacher development in international collaborative higher education*. Retrieved from https://www.igi-global.com/chapter/intramuscular-approach-teacher-development-international/78129

Teachers' ICT competencies Teachers' ICT competency includes ICT skills with innovations in pedagogy, curriculum, and management. The target is to improve teachers' teaching and student learning, to collaborate with colleagues, and perhaps ultimately to become innovation leaders in their institutions.

Basilotta-Gómez-Pablos, V., Matarranz, M., Casado-Aranda, L. A., & Otto, A. (2022). Teachers' digital competencies in higher education: A systematic literature review. *International Journal of Educational Technology in Higher Education, 19*(1), 1–16.

Teaching competency Teaching competencies are the skills and knowledge that help a teacher be successful in teaching (see Sect. 2.1.2).

Teachmint. (n.d.). *Teaching competencies*. Retrieved May 12, 2022, from https://www.teachmint.com/glossary/t/teaching-competencies/#:~:text=Teaching%20competencies%20are%20the%20skills%20and%20knowledge%20that,deal%20with%20every%20student%20

Technical and Vocational Education and Training (TVET) Technical and Vocational Education and Training' (hereinafter "TVET") is understood as comprising education, training and skills development relating to a wide range of occupational fields, production, services and livelihoods. TVET, as part of lifelong learning, can take place at secondary, post-secondary and tertiary levels and includes work-based learning and continuing training and professional development which may lead to qualifications. TVET also includes a wide range of skills development opportunities attuned to national and local contexts. Learning to learn, the development of literacy and numeracy skills, transversal skills and citizenship skills are integral components of TVET (see Sect. 2.1.1).

UNESCO. (2016). *Technical and vocational education and training (TVET) Recommendation concerning 2015*. Retrieved May 12, 2022, from https://unesdoc.unesco.org/ark:/48223/pf0000245178

The COMET Model COMET refers to "Competence Development and Assessment in TVET". This is a competence diagnostics model that was specifically developed for TVET. It takes into consideration the special features, the diverse and complex requirements and demands of TVET, in terms of competence development and assessment in both the classroom and workplace. Originated in Germany in 2006 and led by Professor Felix Rauner, the COMET project has now been developed into an international research consortium participated by countries such as China and South Africa (Rauner et al., 2013a, 2013b) (see Sect. 2.2.2).

Rauner, F., Heinemann, L., & Hauschildt, U. (2013a). Measuring occupational competences: Concept, method and findings of the COMET project. In L. Deitmer, U. Hauschildt, F. Rauner, & H. Zelloth (Eds.), *The architecture of innovative apprenticeship* (pp. 159–175). Springer Science CBusiness Media.

Rauner, F., Heinemann, L., Maurer, A., Haasler, B., Erdwien, B., & Martens, T. (2013b). *Competence-development and assessment in TVET. theoretical framework and empirical results (COMET)*. Springer Verlag.

Zhong, Z. (2020). *Be a wise teacher of technology empowerment*. Jiangxi Normal University.

The SMART framework Based on smart education ideas, the SMART framework was developed for teacher professional development, which consists of five interrelated constructs represented by S, M, A, R and T. S represents SMART-education idea directed; M refers to Self-managed; A is Adaptive; R stands for Reflective; T means Technology-empowered (see Sect. 2.2.3).

Zhong, Z. (2020). *Be a wise teacher of technology empowerment*. Jiangxi Normal University.

TPACK TPACK stands for Technological, Pedagogical Content Knowledge and it is a framework of technology integration into education. The three main components of teacher knowledge in the framework are content knowledge (CK), pedagogical knowledge (PK), and technological knowledge (TK). The other components, pedagogical and content knowledge (PCK), technological content knowledge (TCK), technological pedagogical knowledge (TPK), and TPACK, are knowledge developed through the interactions between and among these three core bodies of knowledge (see Sect. 2.2.1).

Koehler, M. J., & Mishra, P. (2005). What happens when teachers design educational technology? The development of technological pedagogical content knowledge. *Journal of Educational Computing Research, 32*, 131–152.

TVET teacher professional development In this handbook, TVET teacher professional development is defined as the continuing learning by in-service TVET teachers to upgrade professional skills, knowledge and disposition in order to enhance career progression, to keep up with demands from industry and technological advancements and to stay current with professional regulatory requirements (see Sect. 2.1.2).

TVET teachers The main clusters of TVET teachers are − Teachers or lecturers working in formal vocational school or college settings and delivering vocational courses. − Instructors and laboratory assistants working in school or college settings in vocational training facilities. − Others who teach with a high degree of autonomy or sometimes act as assistants to other vocational teachers. − Trainers, tutors and others in enterprises who integrate training and education functions into their jobs with varying degrees (from incidental to full-time teaching of trainees and apprentices). In dual systems, this function is often separated from HRD functions within companies, while in others this distinction is not strongly maintained. − Instructors and trainers working in labour market training institutions supported by governments and/or public authorities, often with a strong focus on social inclusion and basic occupational competences; − Instructors and trainers working in organizations, such as chambers of commerce, sectoral training institutions or privately-run training companies and providers that focus on upgrading technical competences, training in communication skills, etc.

Grollmann, P., & Rauner, F. (2007). TVET teachers: An endangered species or professional innovation agents? In P. Grollmann, & F. Rauner, (Eds.), *International perspectives on teachers and lecturers in technical and vocational education. UNESCO-UNEVOC book series technical and vocational education and training: Issues, concerns and prospects* (vol. 7, pp. 6–7). Springer.

The manufacturer's authorised representative in the EU is Springer Nature Customer Service Centre GmbH, Europaplatz 3, 69115 Heidelberg, Germany. If you have any concerns regarding our products, please contact ProductSafety@springernature.com

Printed and bound by CPI Group (UK) Ltd, Croydon, CR0 4YY

25/03/2026

02078170-0013